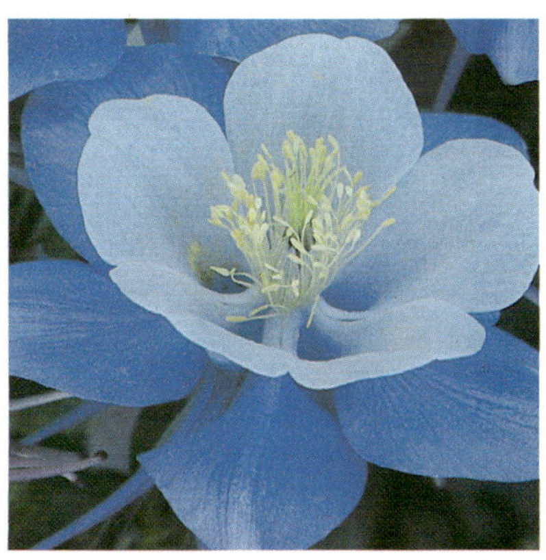

PORTRAIT OF
COLORADO

Portrait of America Series

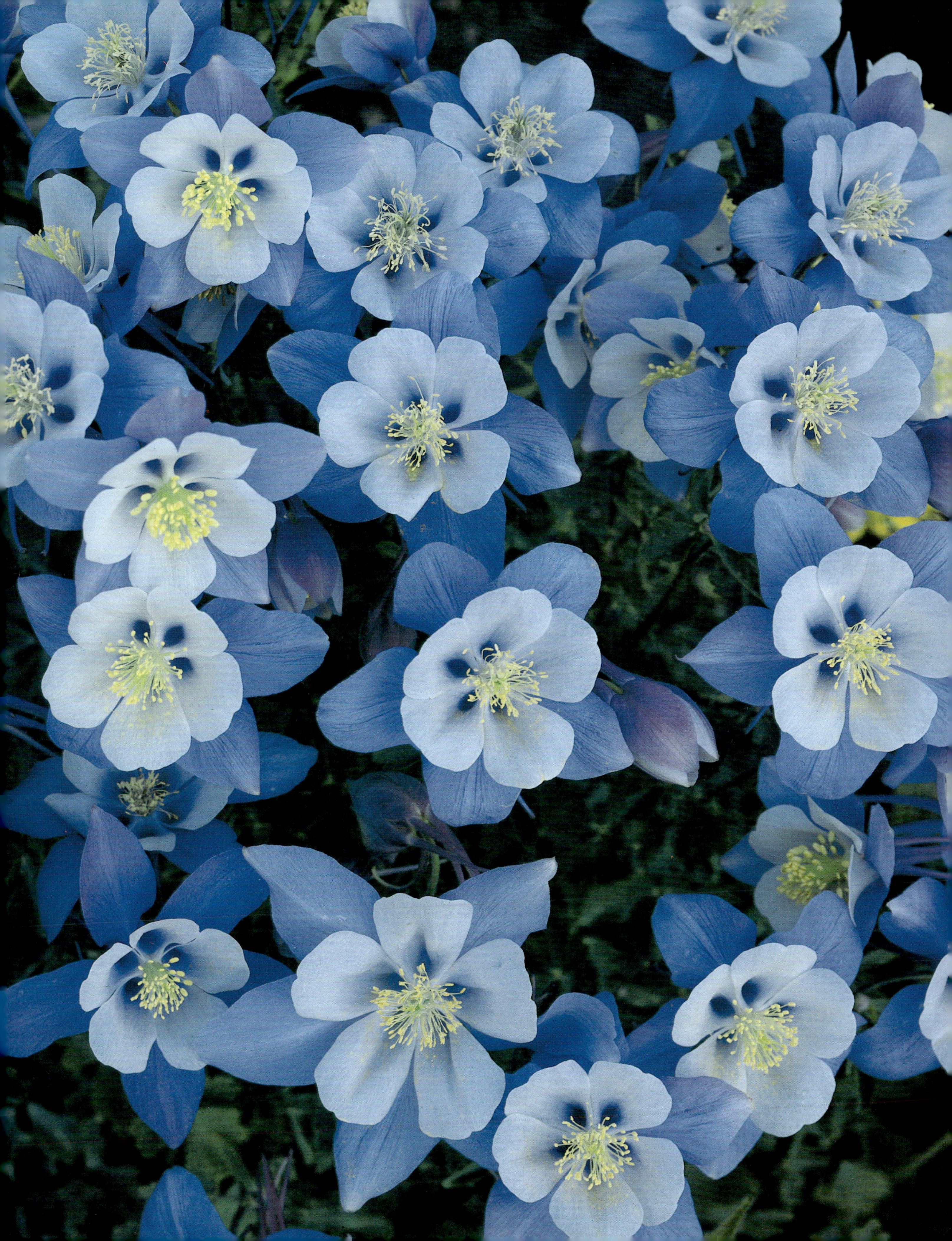

PORTRAIT OF
COLORADO
DAVID MUENCH

TEXT BY DAVID SUMNER

GRAPHIC ARTS CENTER PUBLISHING™

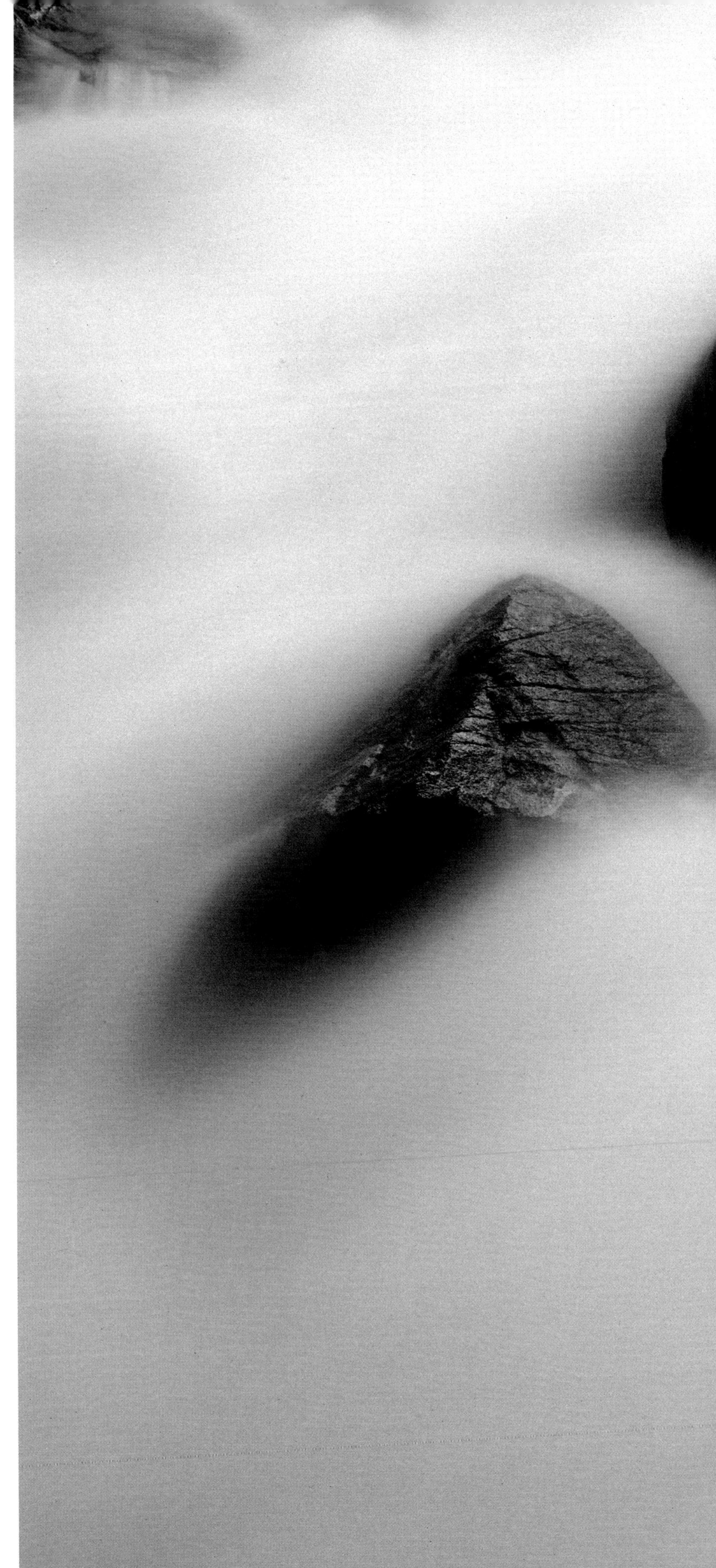

ISBN 1-55868-102-7
Library of Congress Catalog No. 93-78467
Copyright © MCMXCIII by
Graphic Arts Center Publishing Company
P.O. Box 10306
Portland, OR 97210
503/226-2402

President • Charles M. Hopkins
Editor-in-Chief • Douglas Pfeiffer
Managing Editor • Jean Andrews
Designer • Bonnie Muench
Production Manager • Richard L. Owsiany
Typographer • Harrison Typesetting, Inc.
Printer • Dynagraphics, Inc.
Binding • Lincoln & Allen
Printed in the United States of America

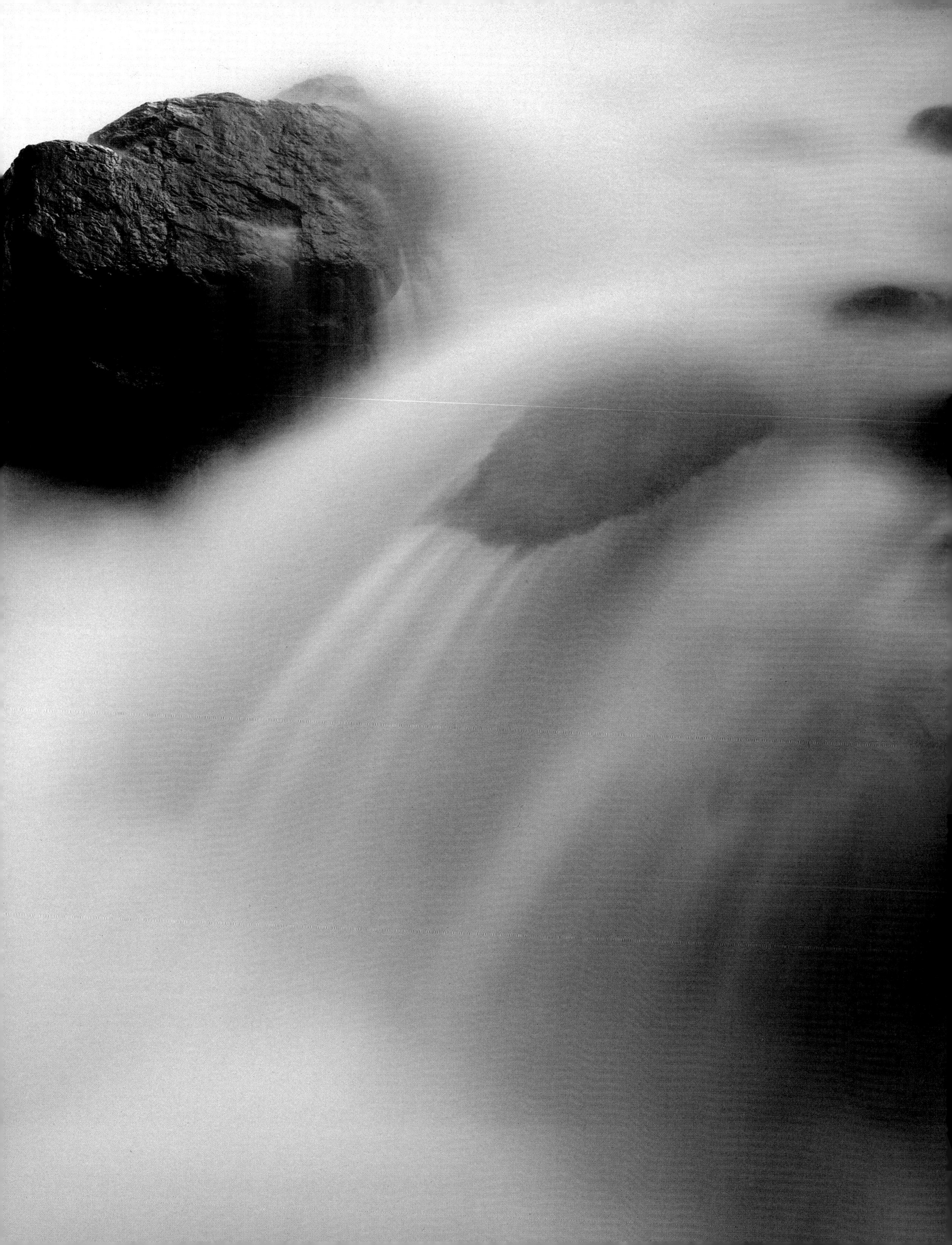

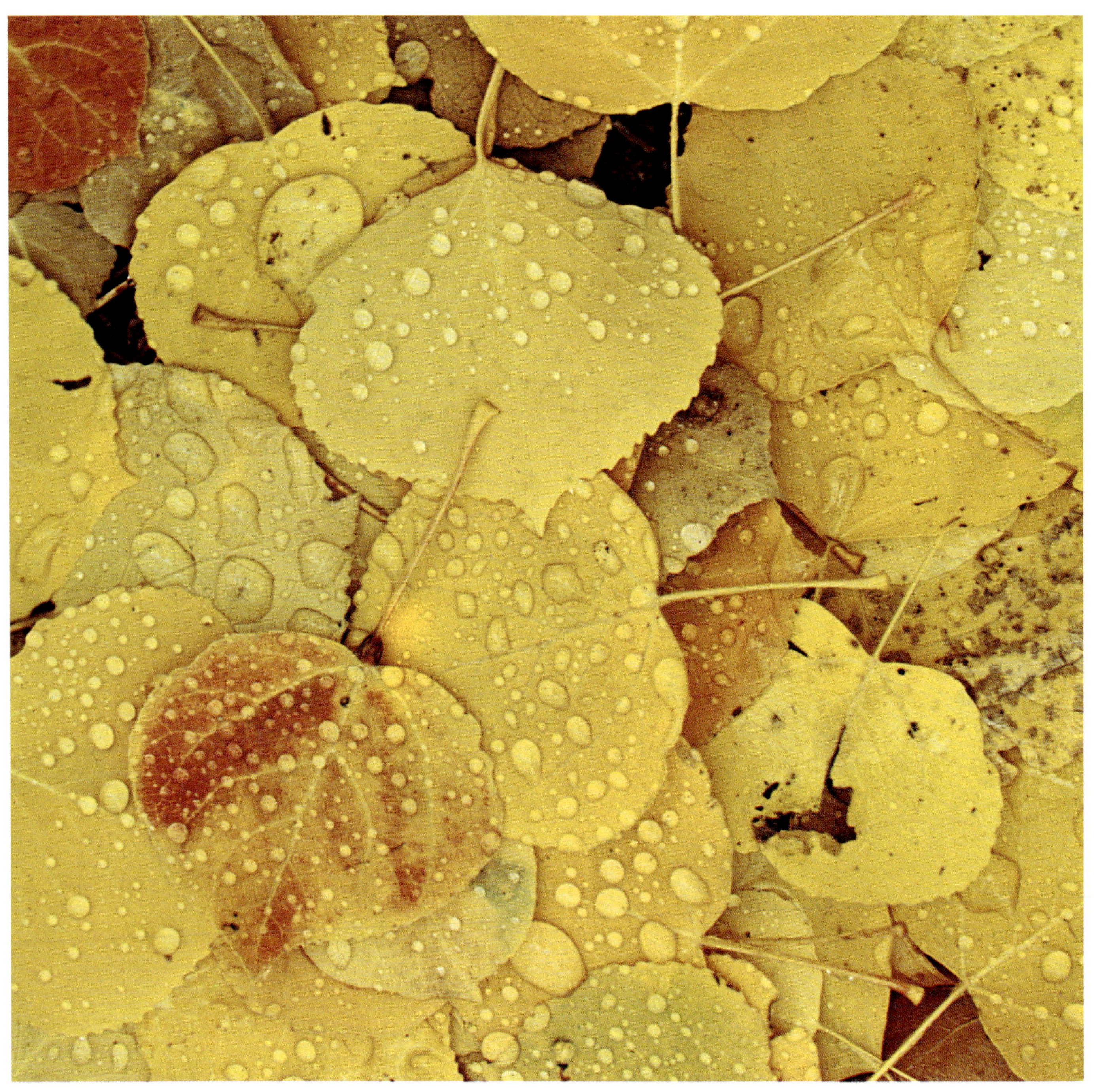

▲ Fragile, short-lived aspen leaves create an elegant pattern on the forest floor near Engineer Pass.
▶ Spring snow melts from Mount Elbert's summit.

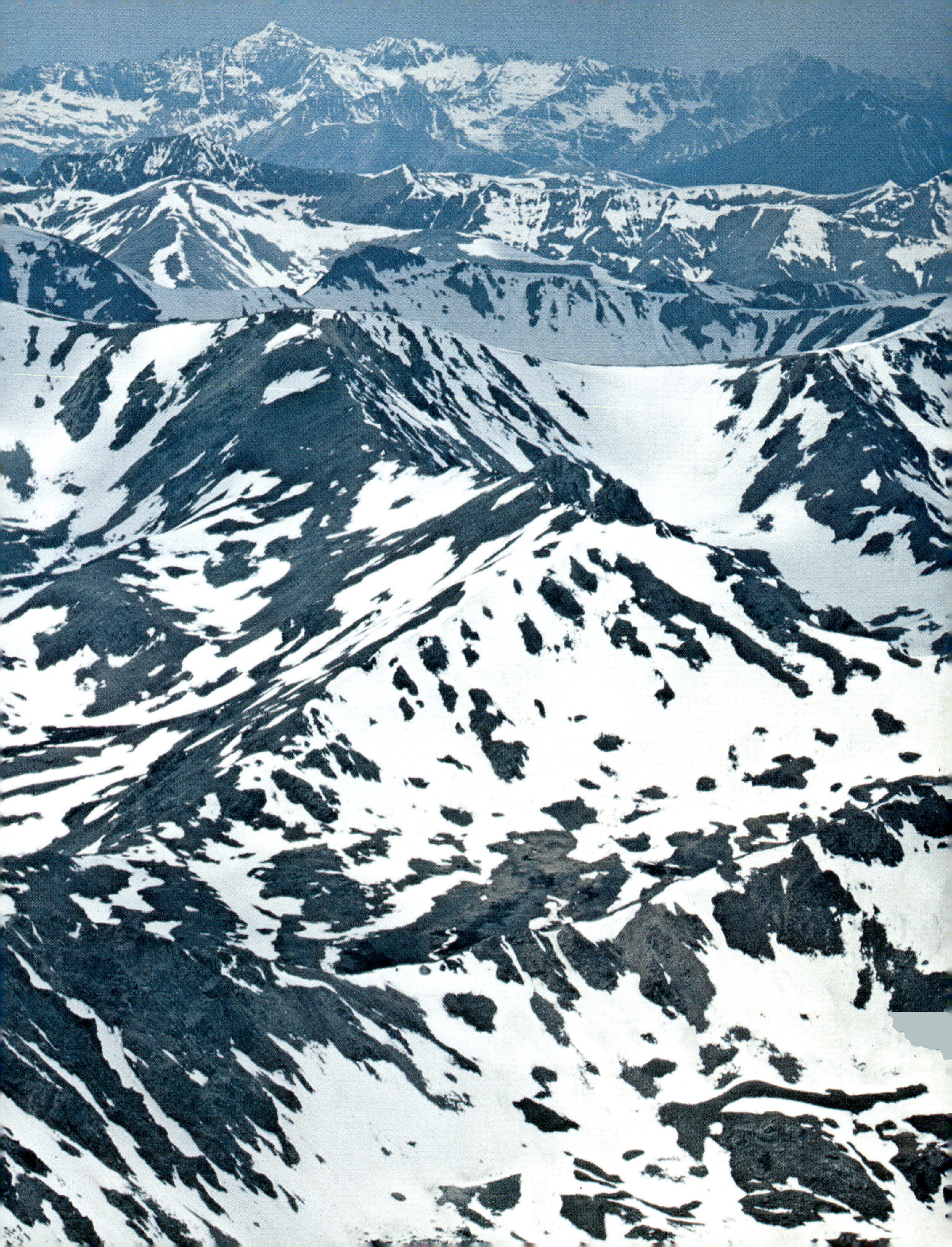

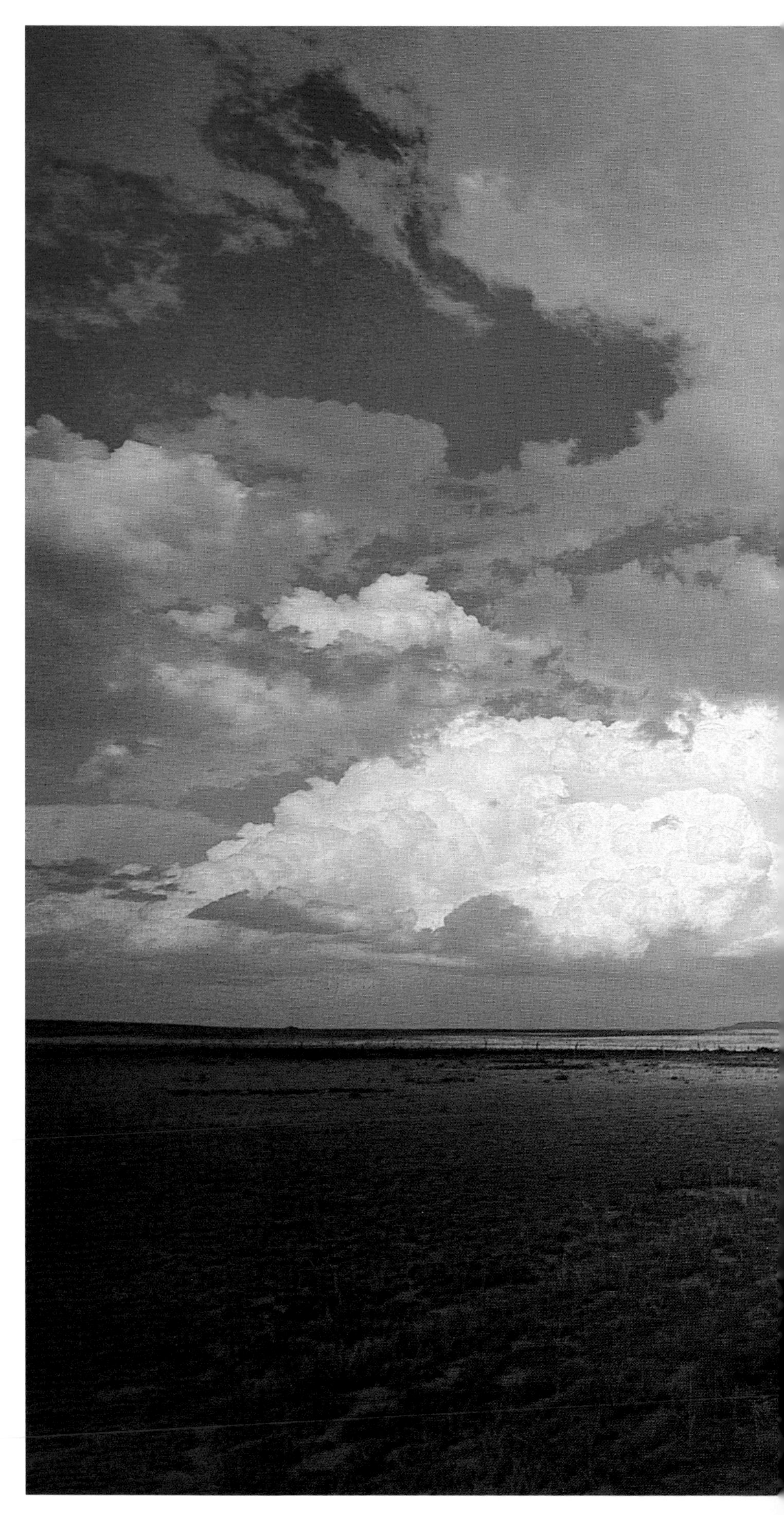

THE
PLAINS

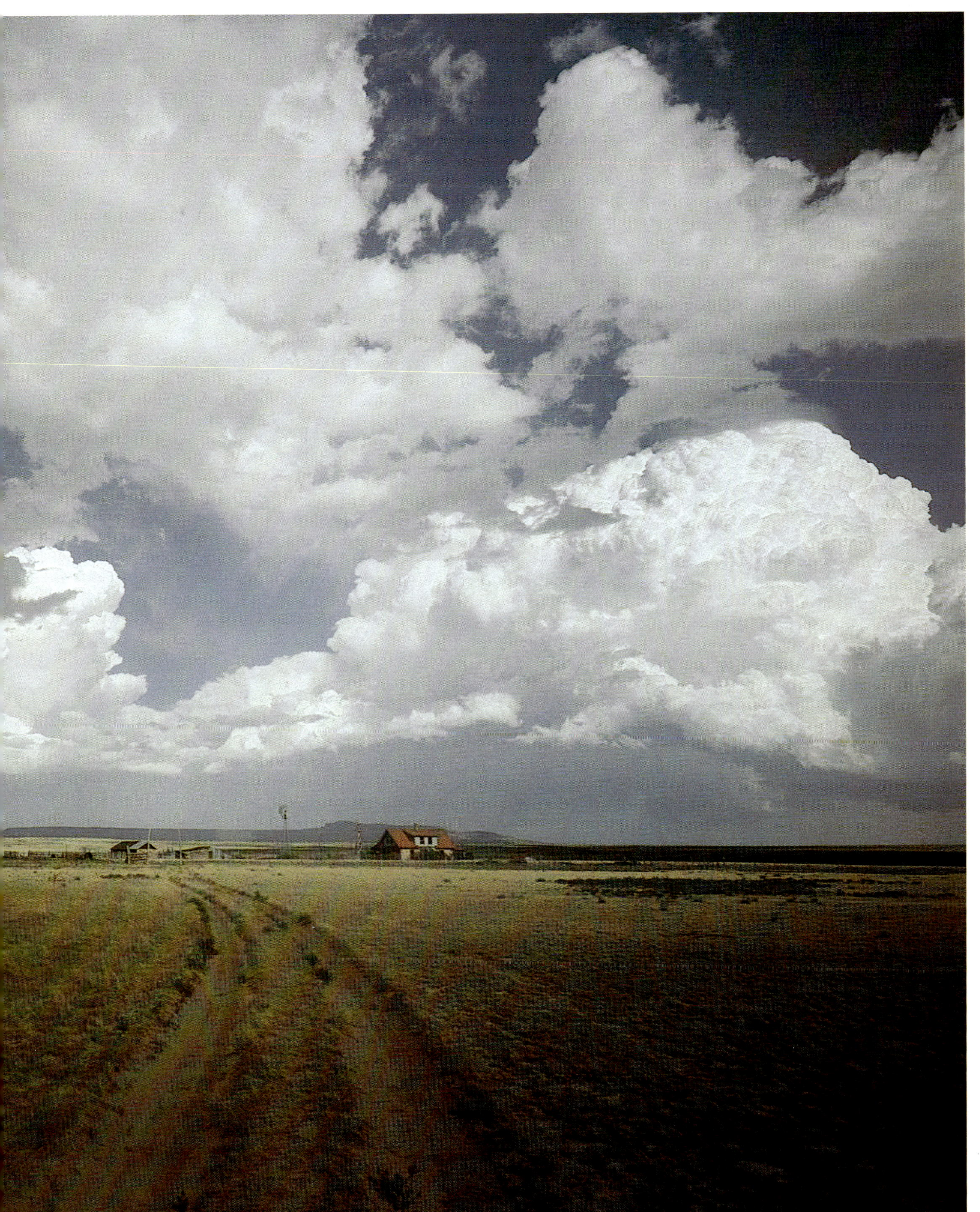

▲ Cumulus clouds bring hope for rain beneath Mesa de Maya, east of Trinidad.

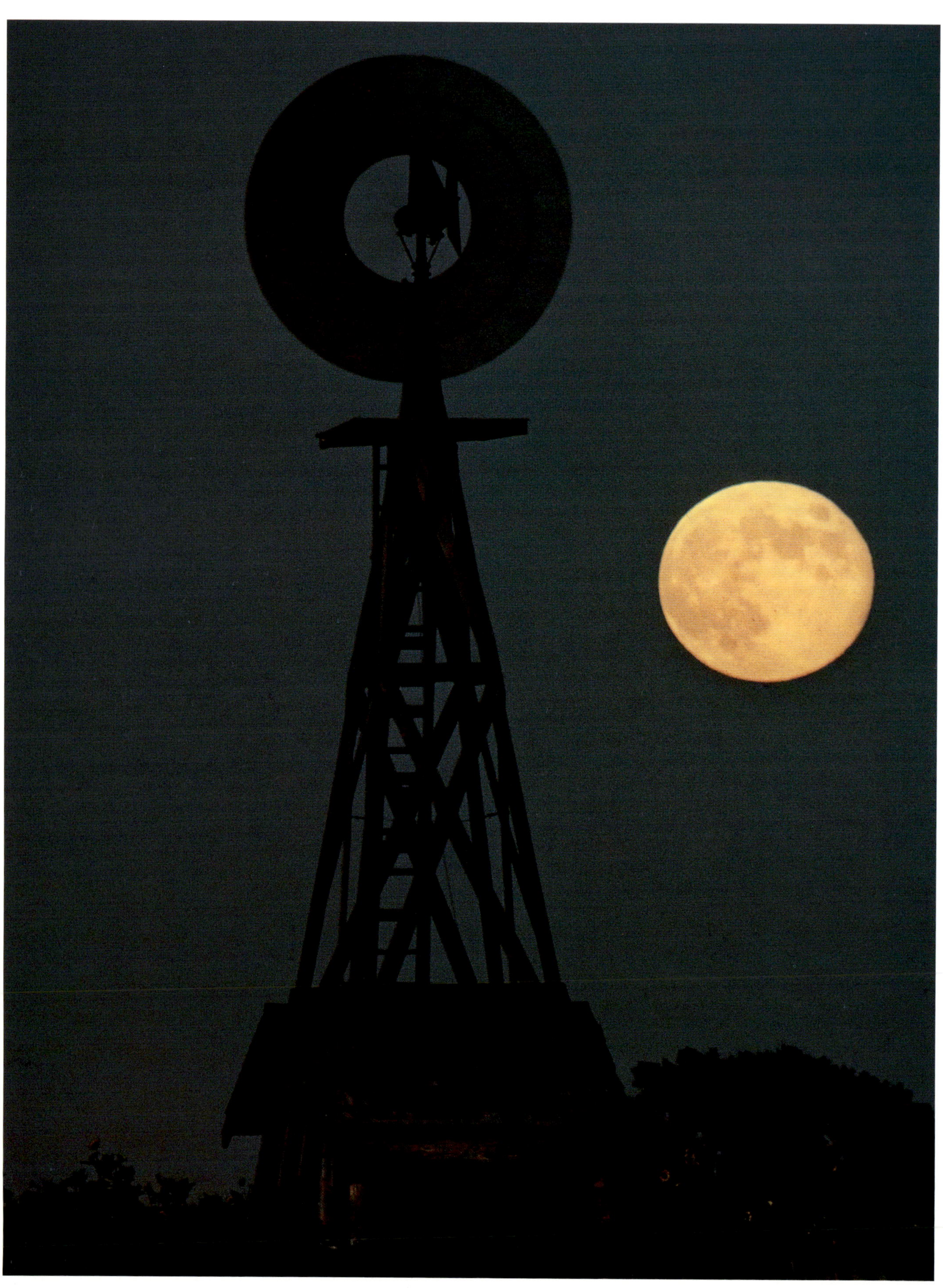

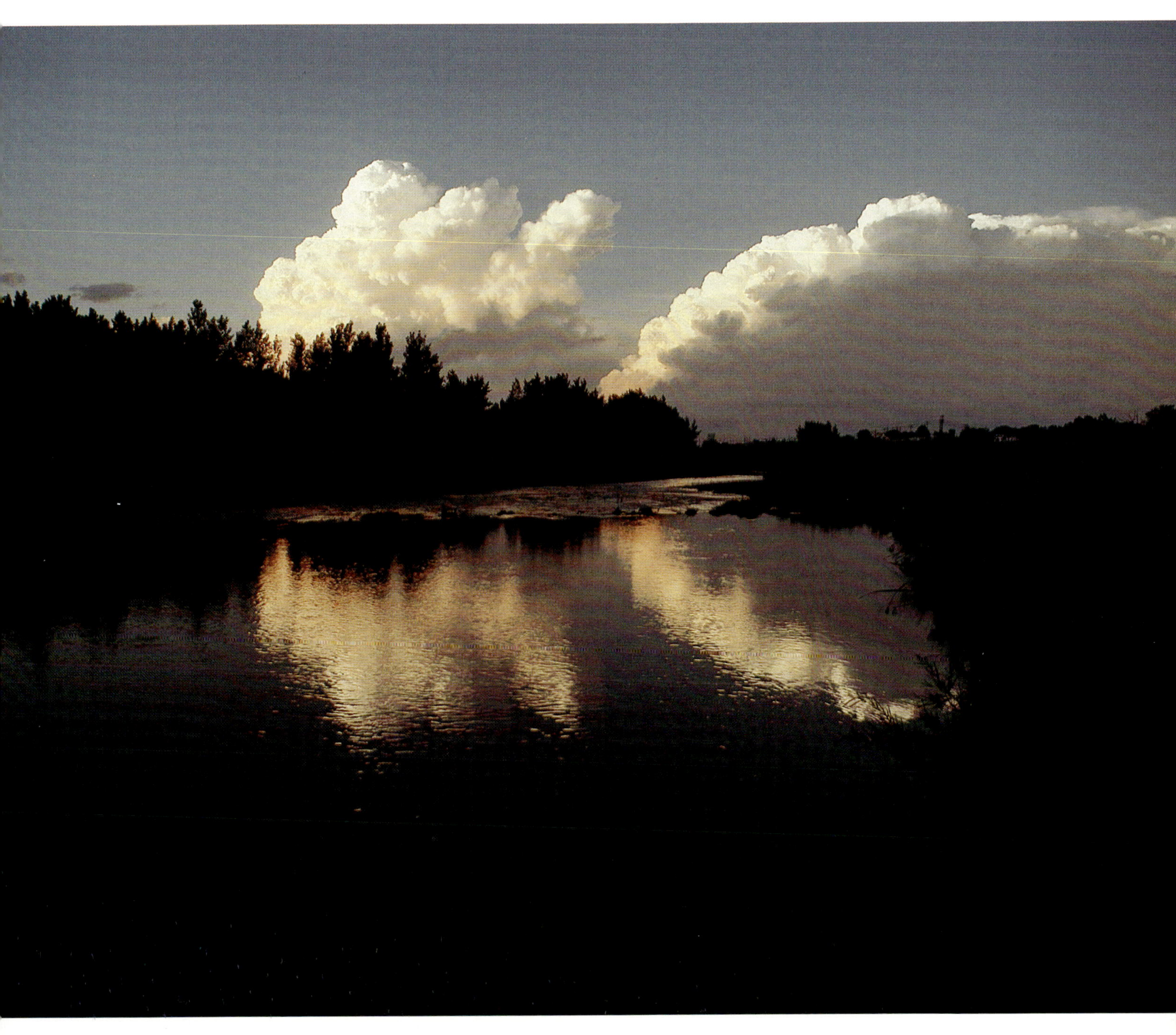

◄ A full moon highlights an old windmill on the plains east of Punkin Center and west of Cheyenne Wells.
▲ A quiet pool of Purgatoire River, Trinidad, reflects bright clouds.

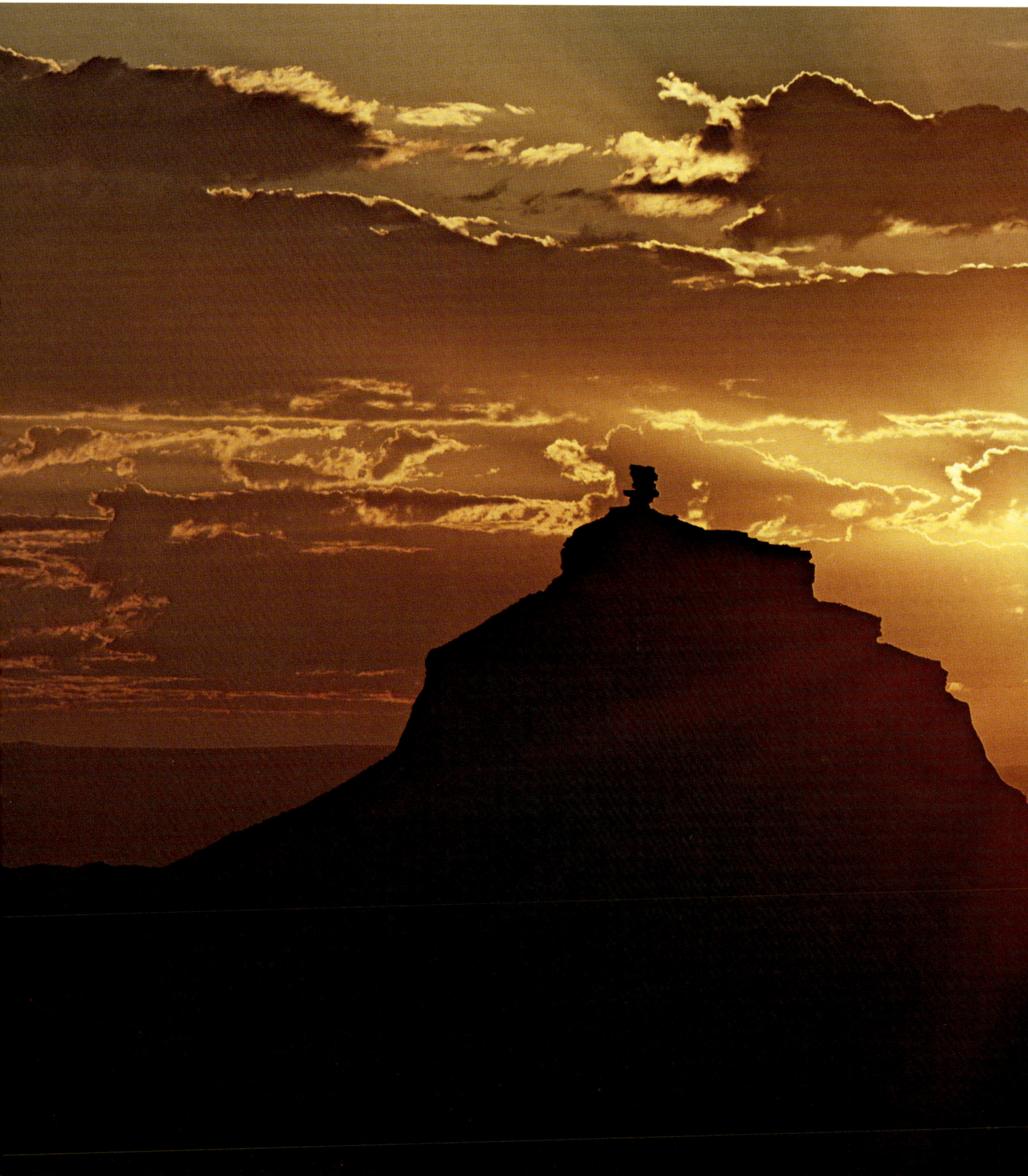

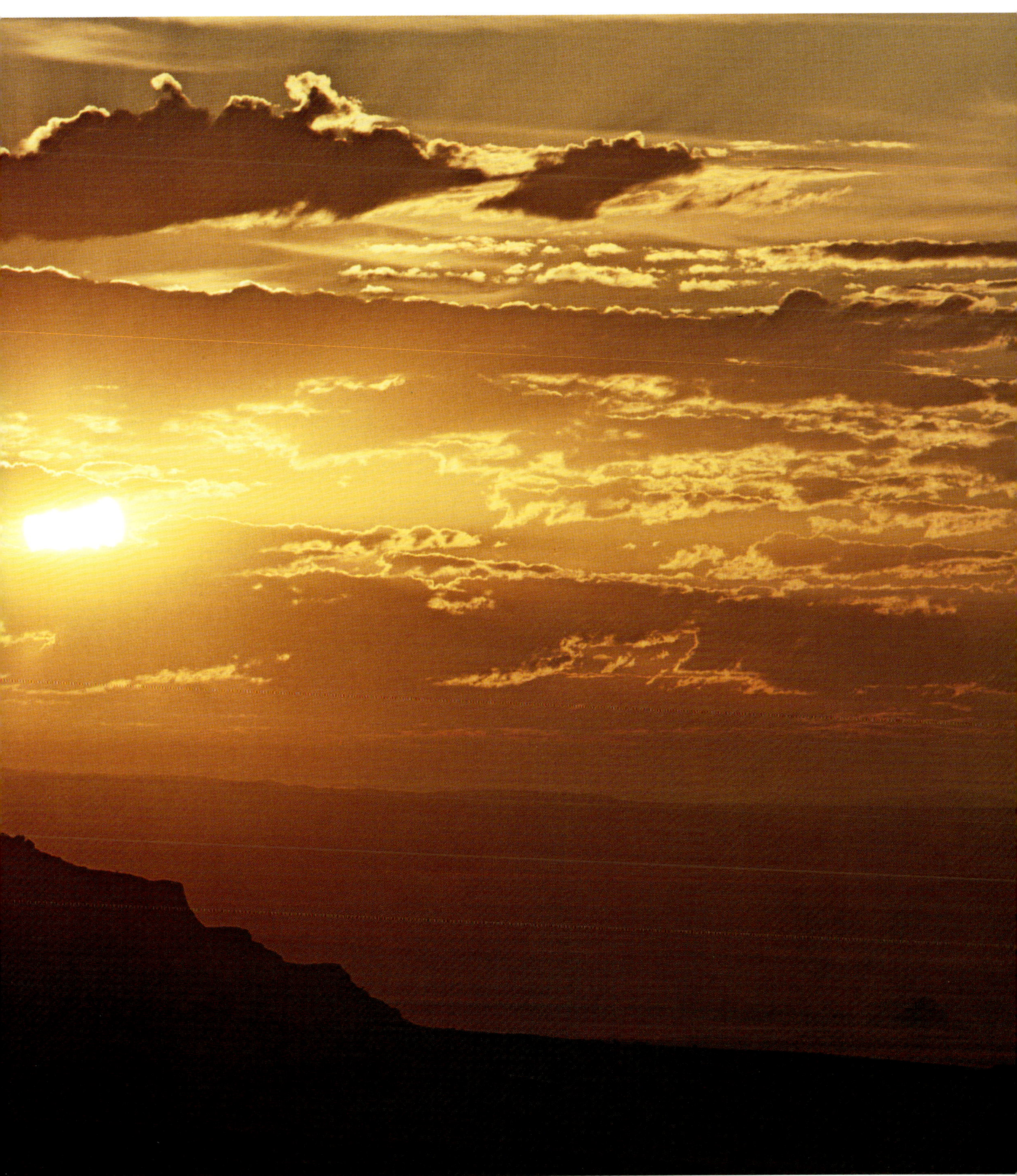

▲ Remnants of Oligocene and Miocene sedimentary buttes rise above Pawnee National Grasslands.

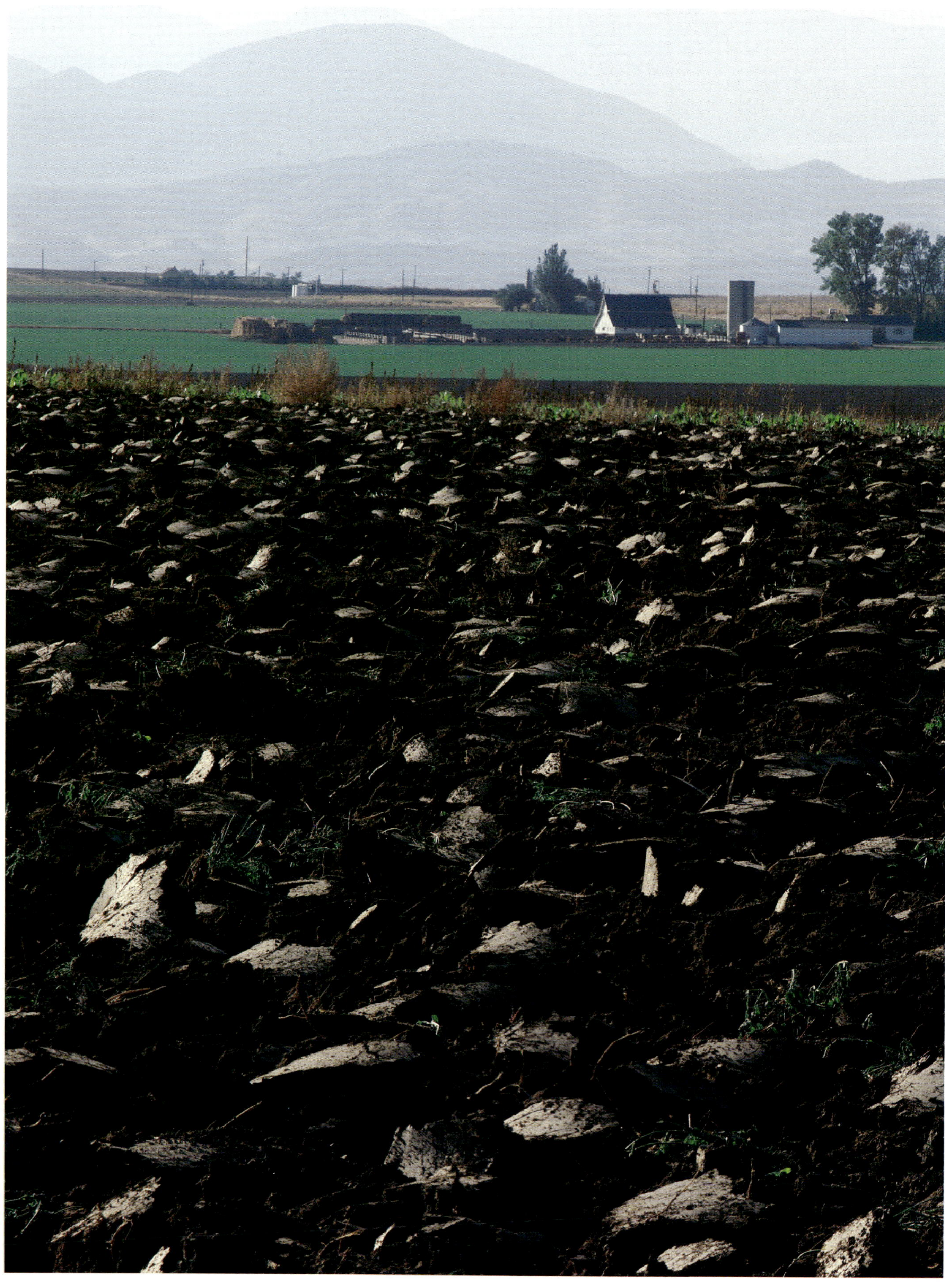

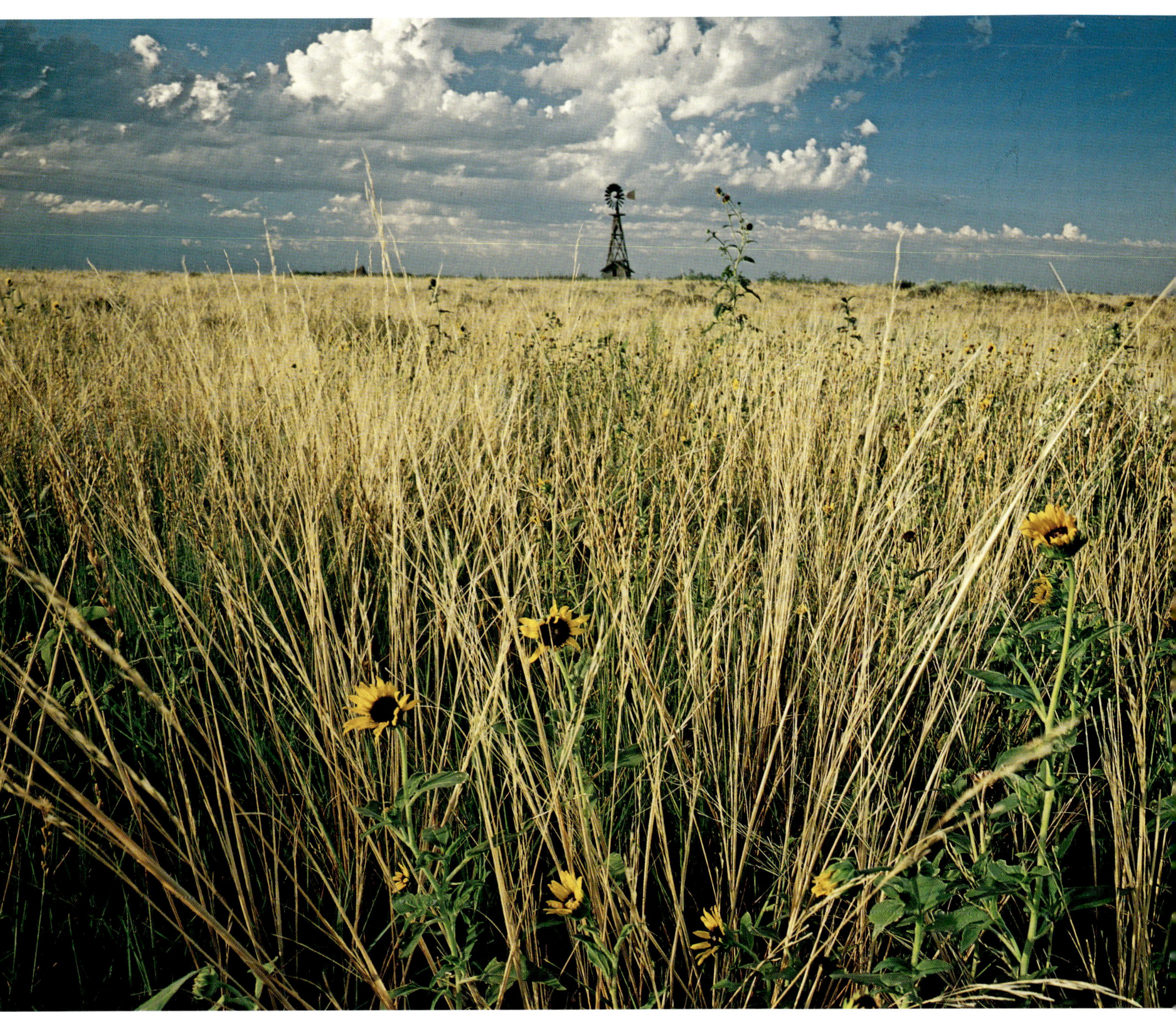

◄ A rich loam on the peneplain attracts tillers of the soil below the Front Range, near Longmont.
▲ Comanche National Grasslands is only a remnant of the once-vast robe covering the great plains.

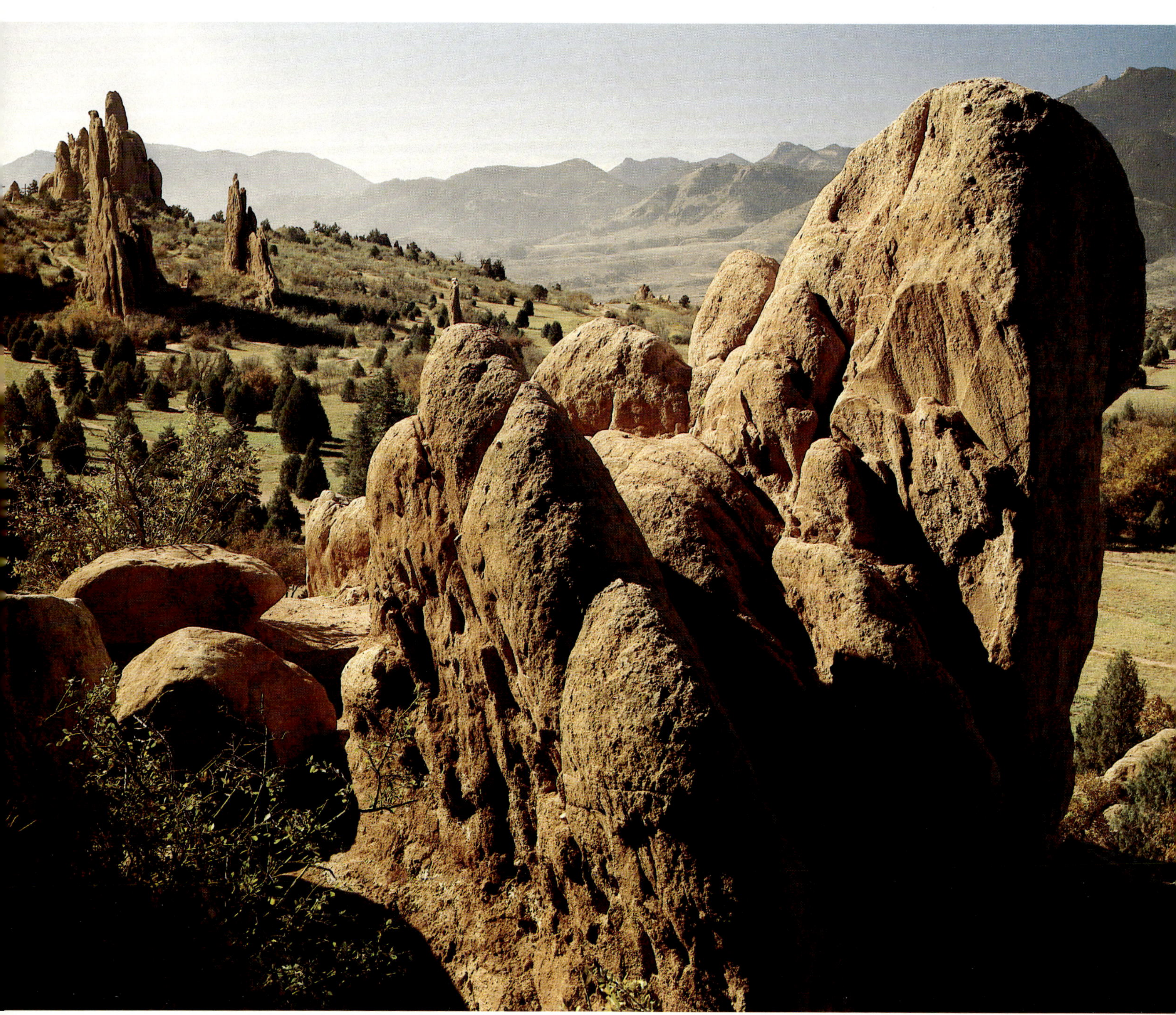

▲ Garden of the Gods, near Colorado Springs, gives strange and muted testimony to a primordial past.

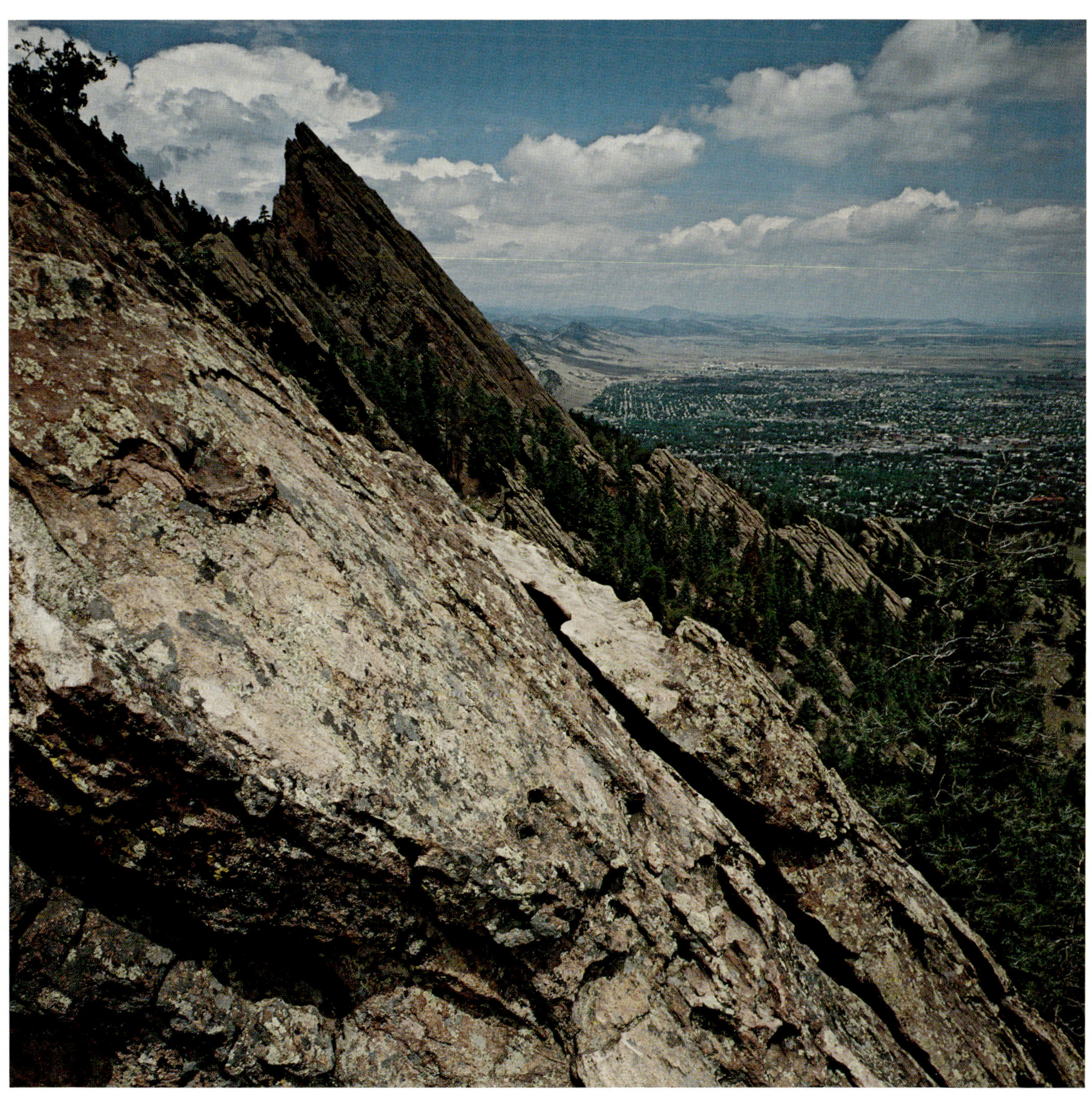

▲ At the edge of the plains, the city of Boulder seems dwarfed by the 3,000-foot-high Flatirons of the Front Range.

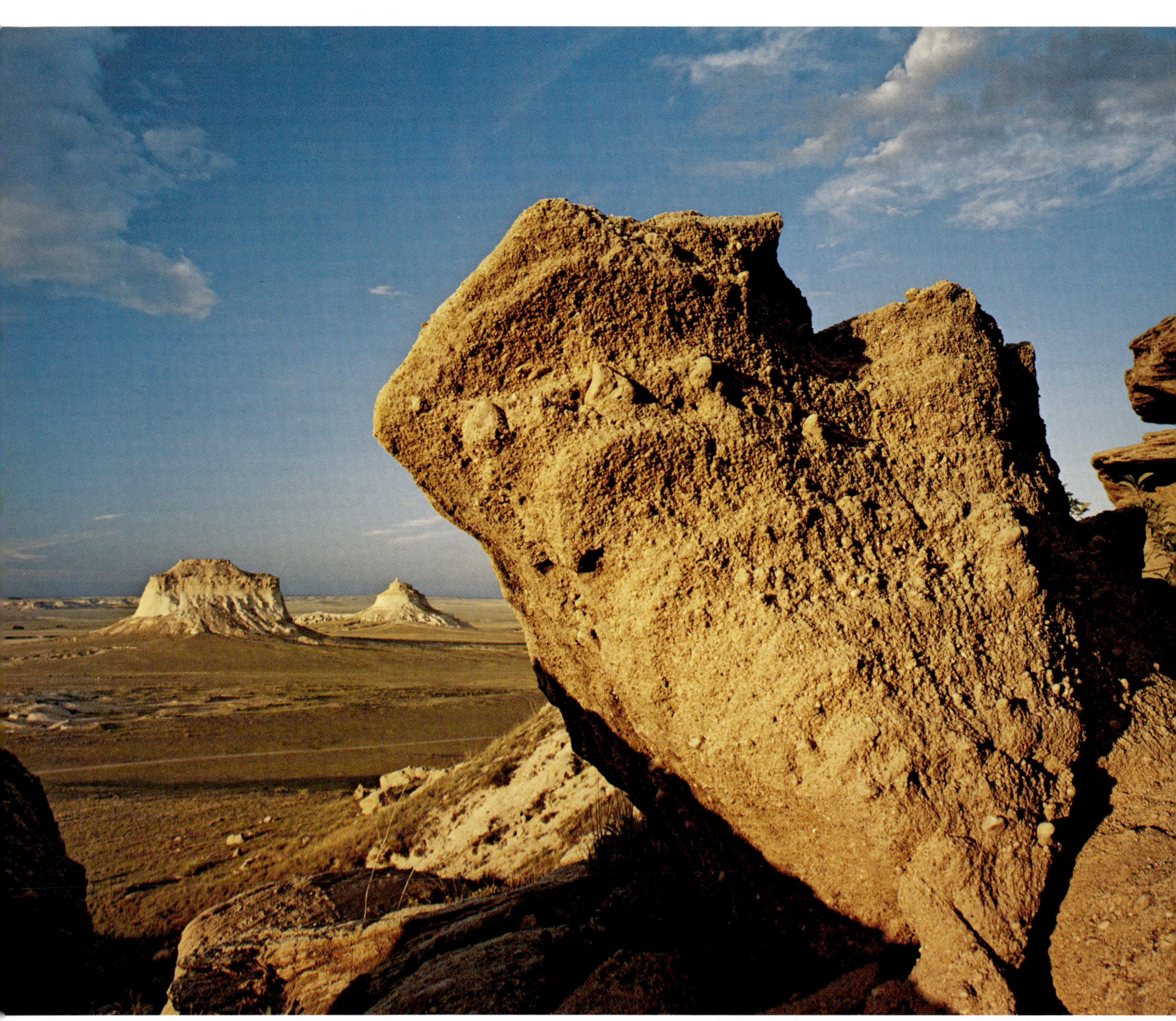

▲ Pawnee Buttes, with its strange rock formations, is situated near the northeast corner of the state.

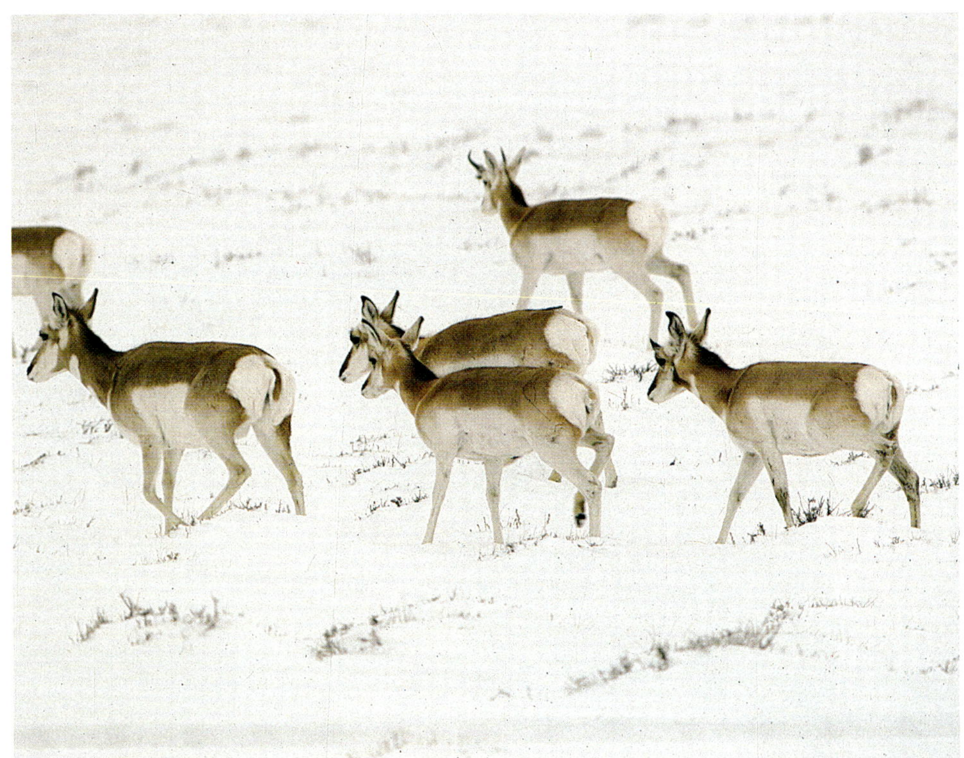

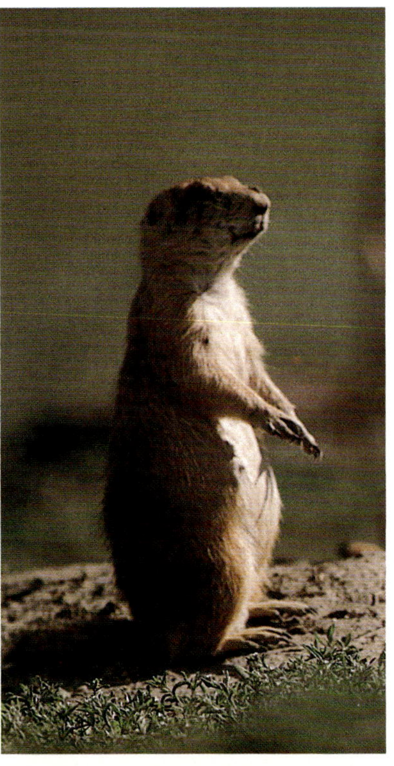

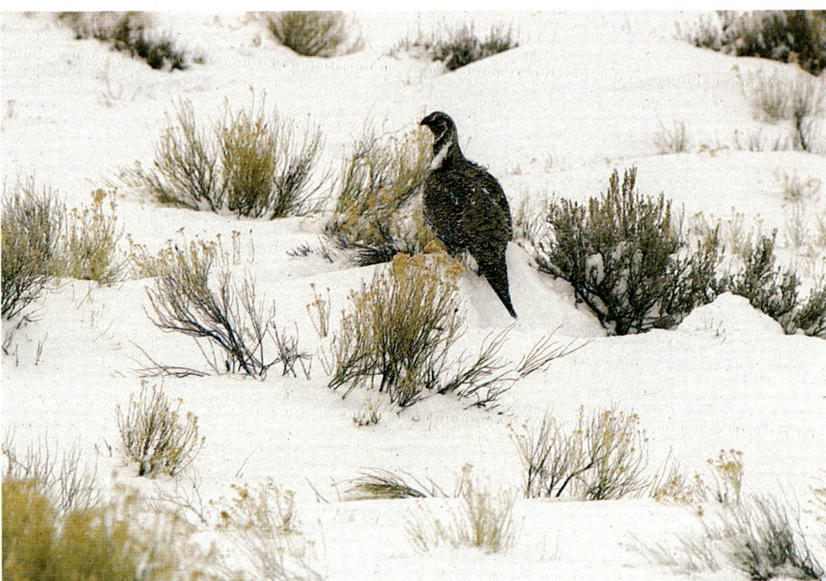

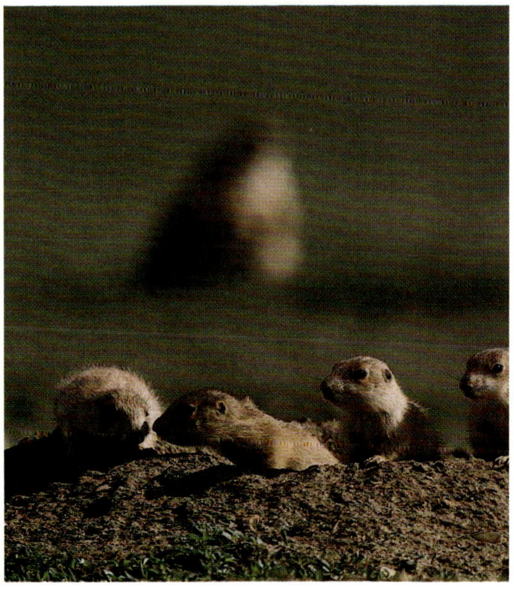

▲ The prairie supports diverse wildlife: pronghorns, prairie dogs, and grouse, among others.

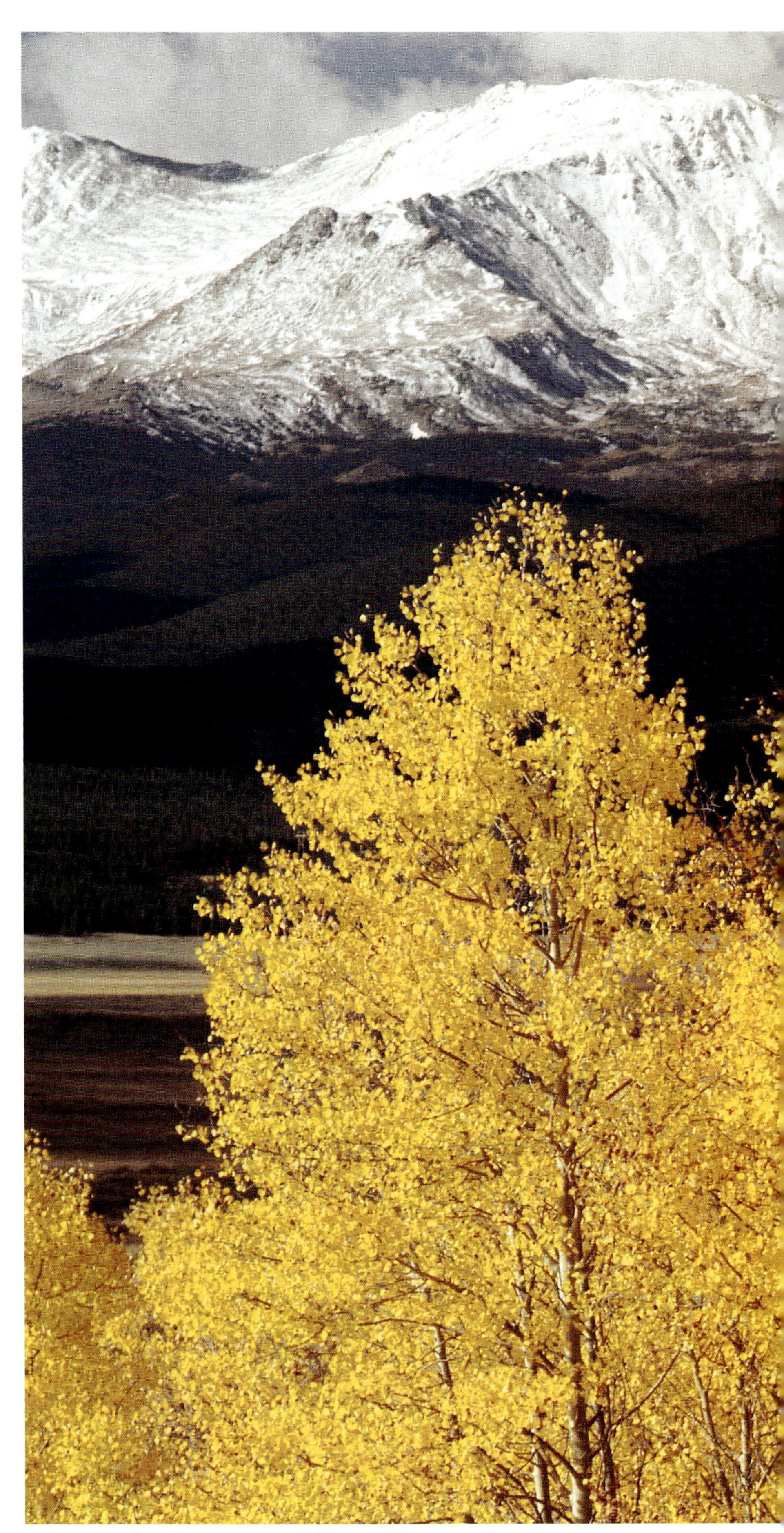

THE
MOUNTAINS

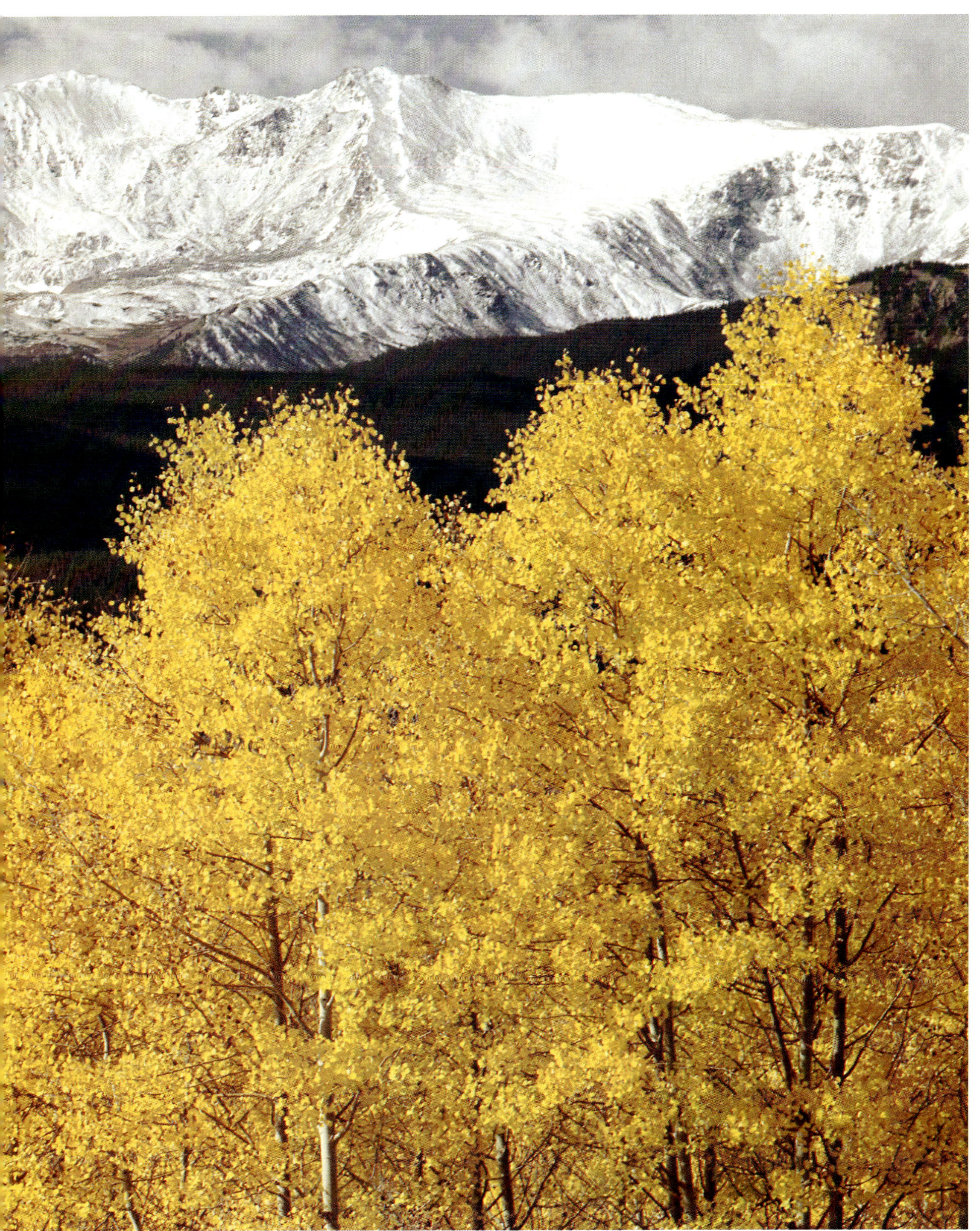

▲ A part of the Sawatch Range, Mount Massive's multiple summit reaches 14,421 feet.

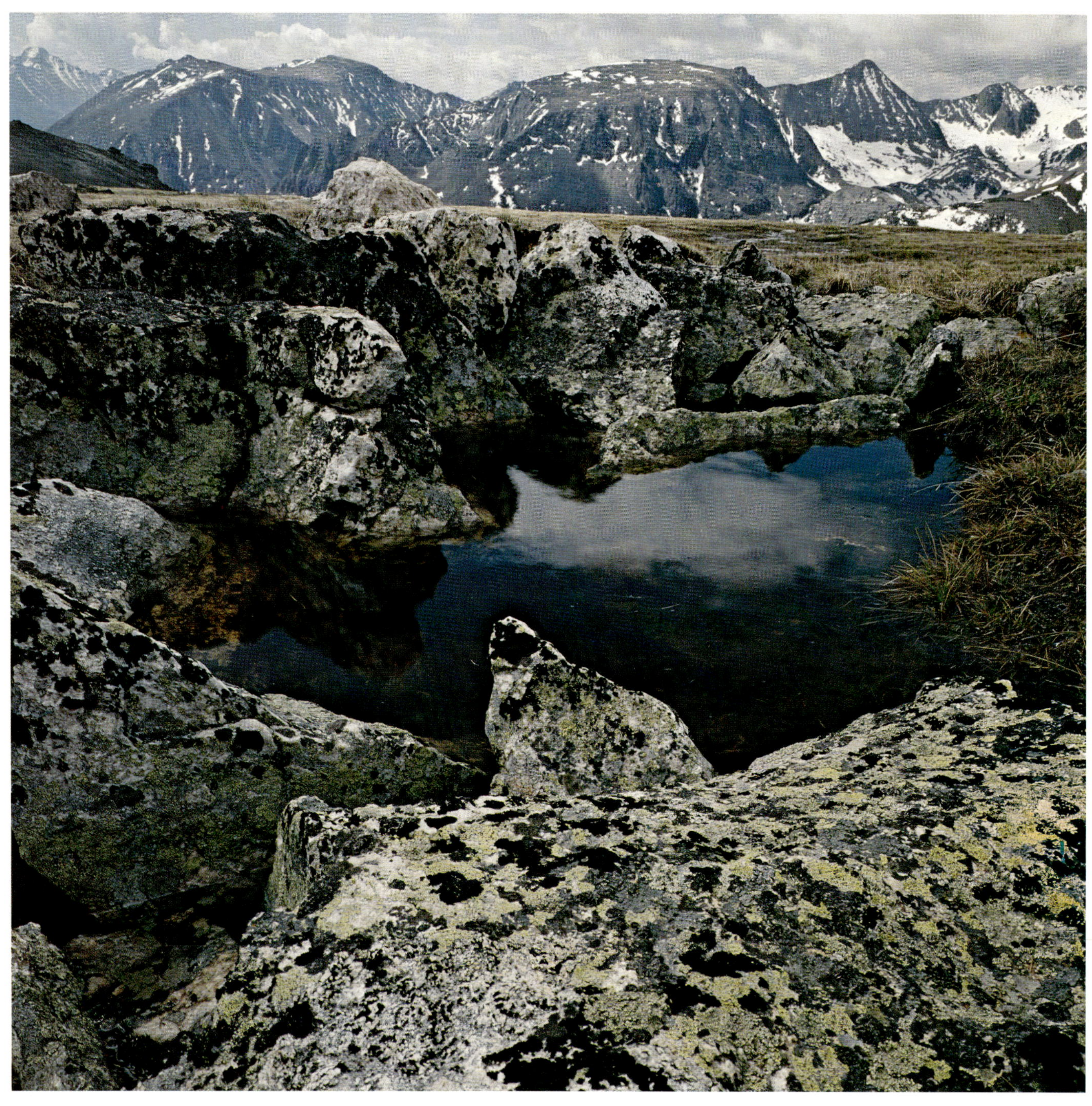

▲ Along Trail Ridge, in Rocky Mountain National Park, ice melt temporarily forms a lichen-coated pond.
► The tumbledown flow of the Crystal River is fed by snowmelt high in the West Elk Range.

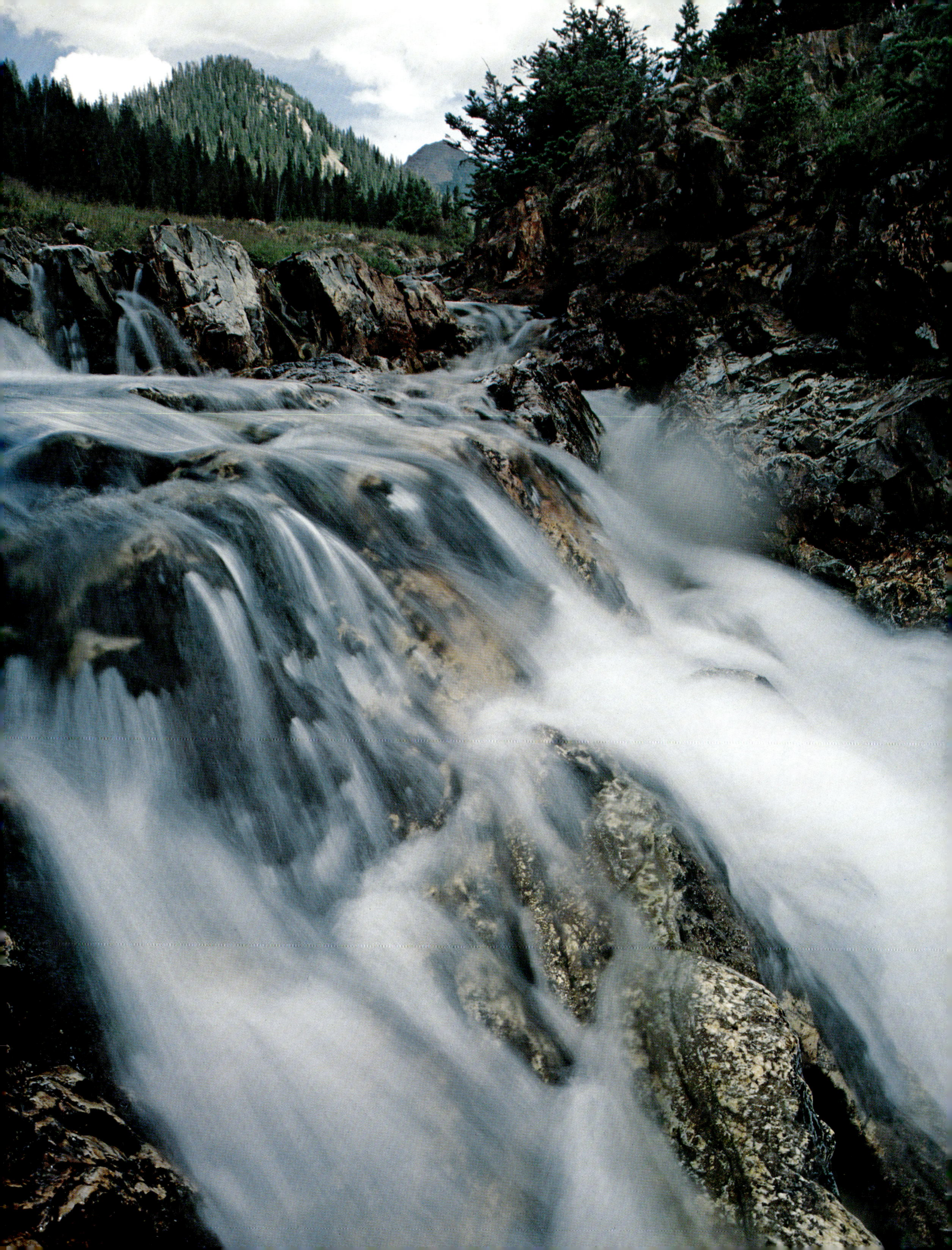

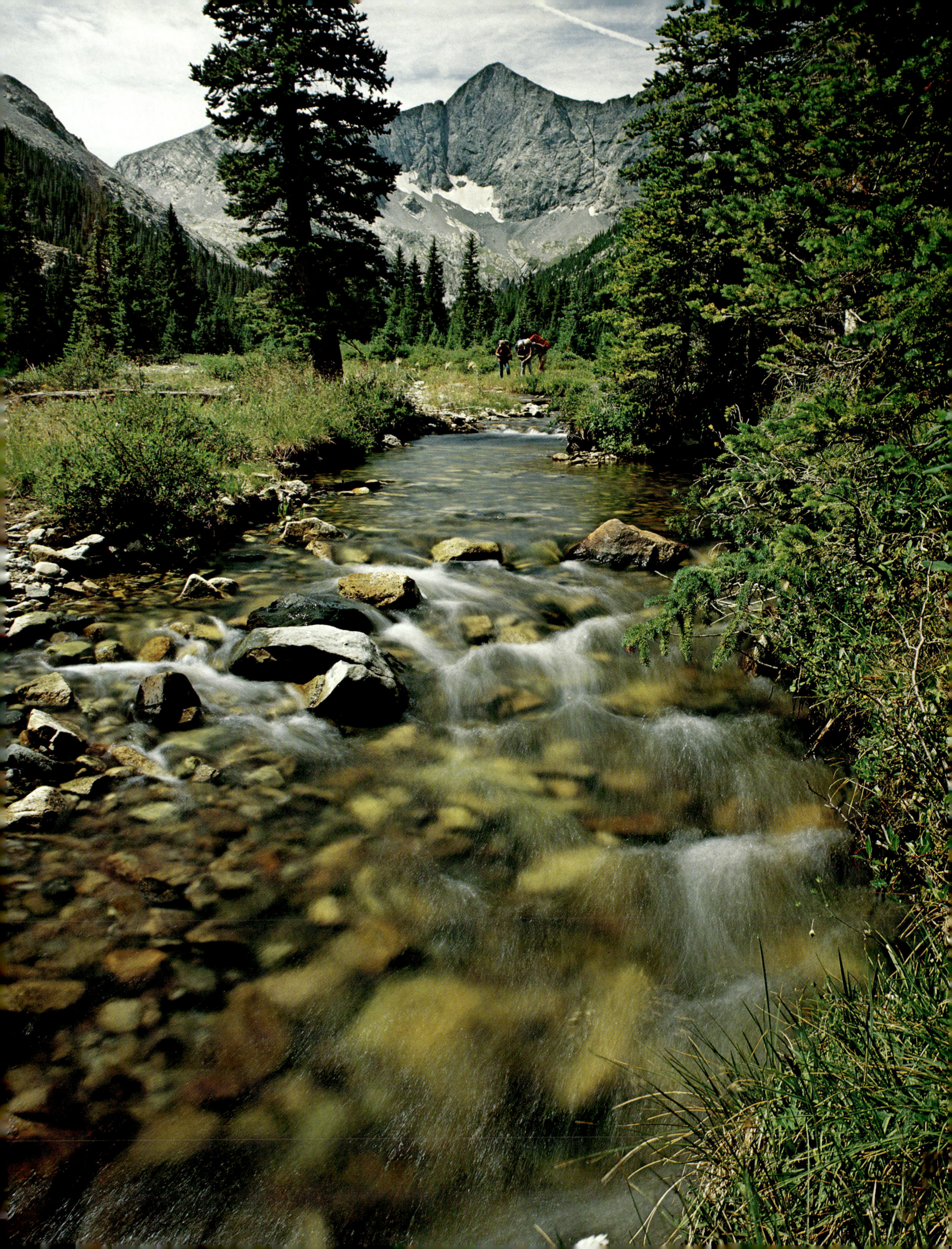

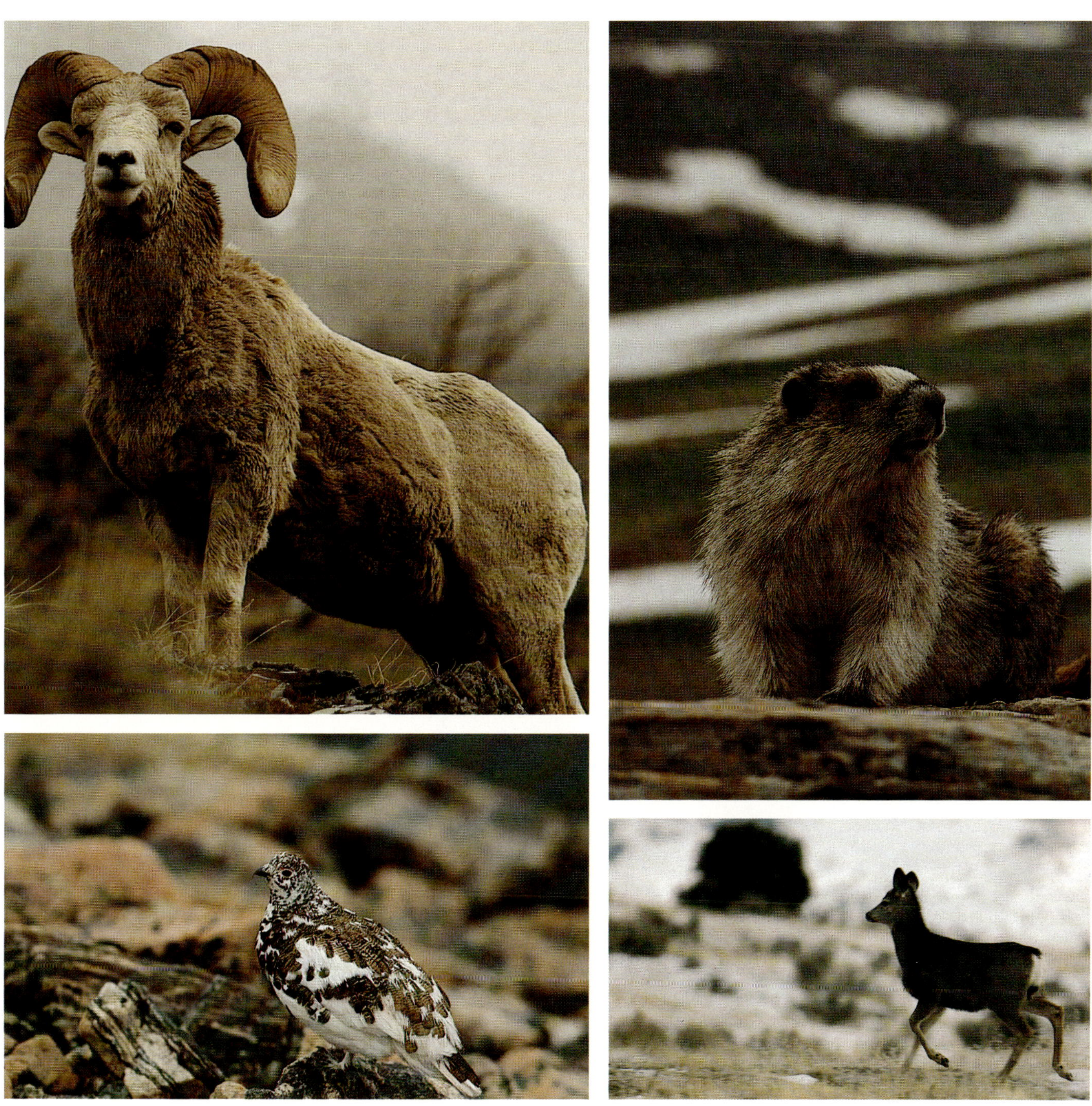

◄ Blanca Peak rises above summer flow of Huerfano River, Lily Lake trail, Sangre de Cristo Range.
▲ Wildlife in mountain areas includes bighorn sheep, marmots, white-tailed ptarmigans, and white-tailed deer.

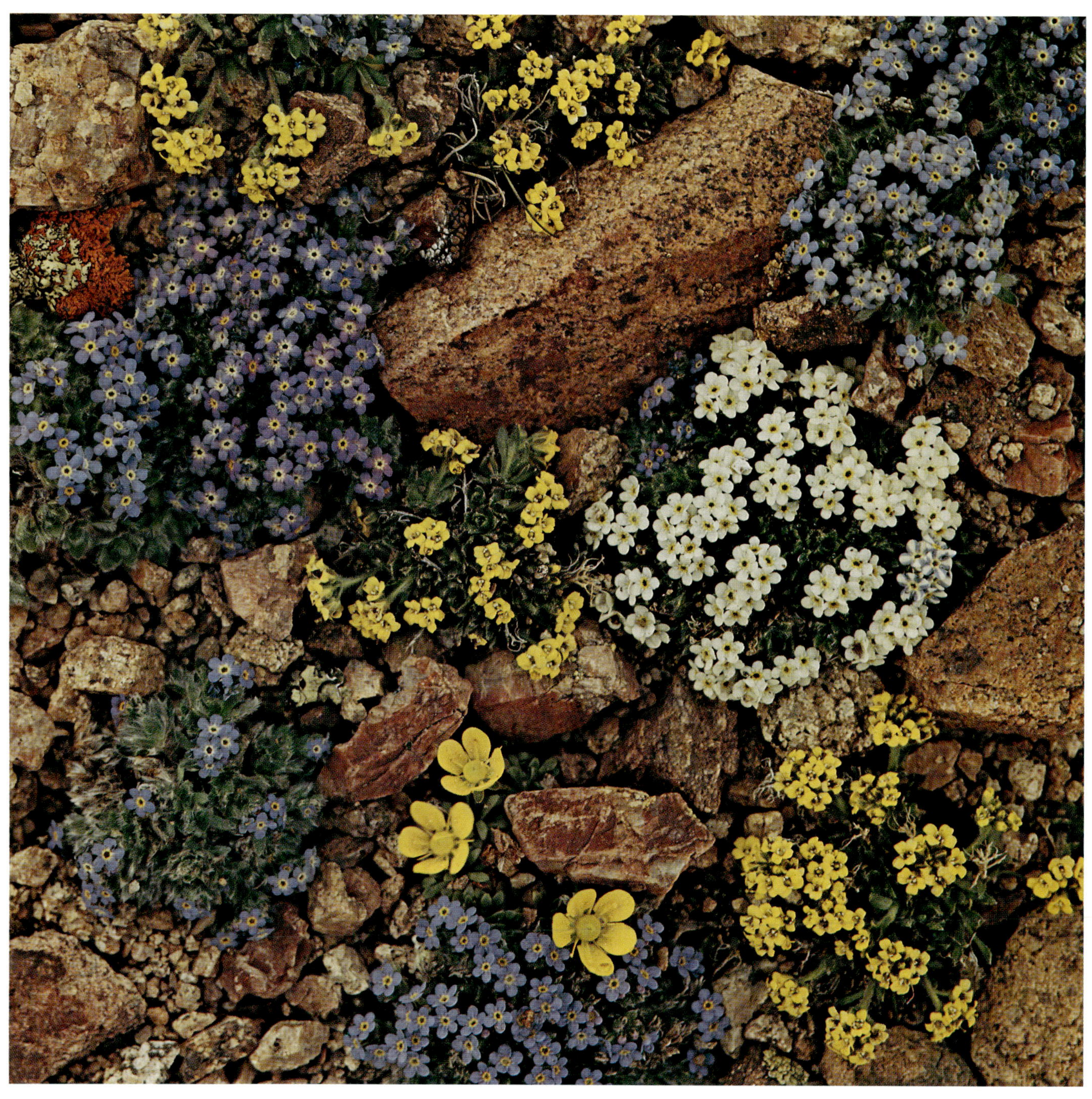

▲ At the 14,000-foot level, an alpine ecosystem displays buttercups and forget-me-nots.
► In the West Elk Mountains, water in the upper Crystal River cascades down cliffs and over rocks.

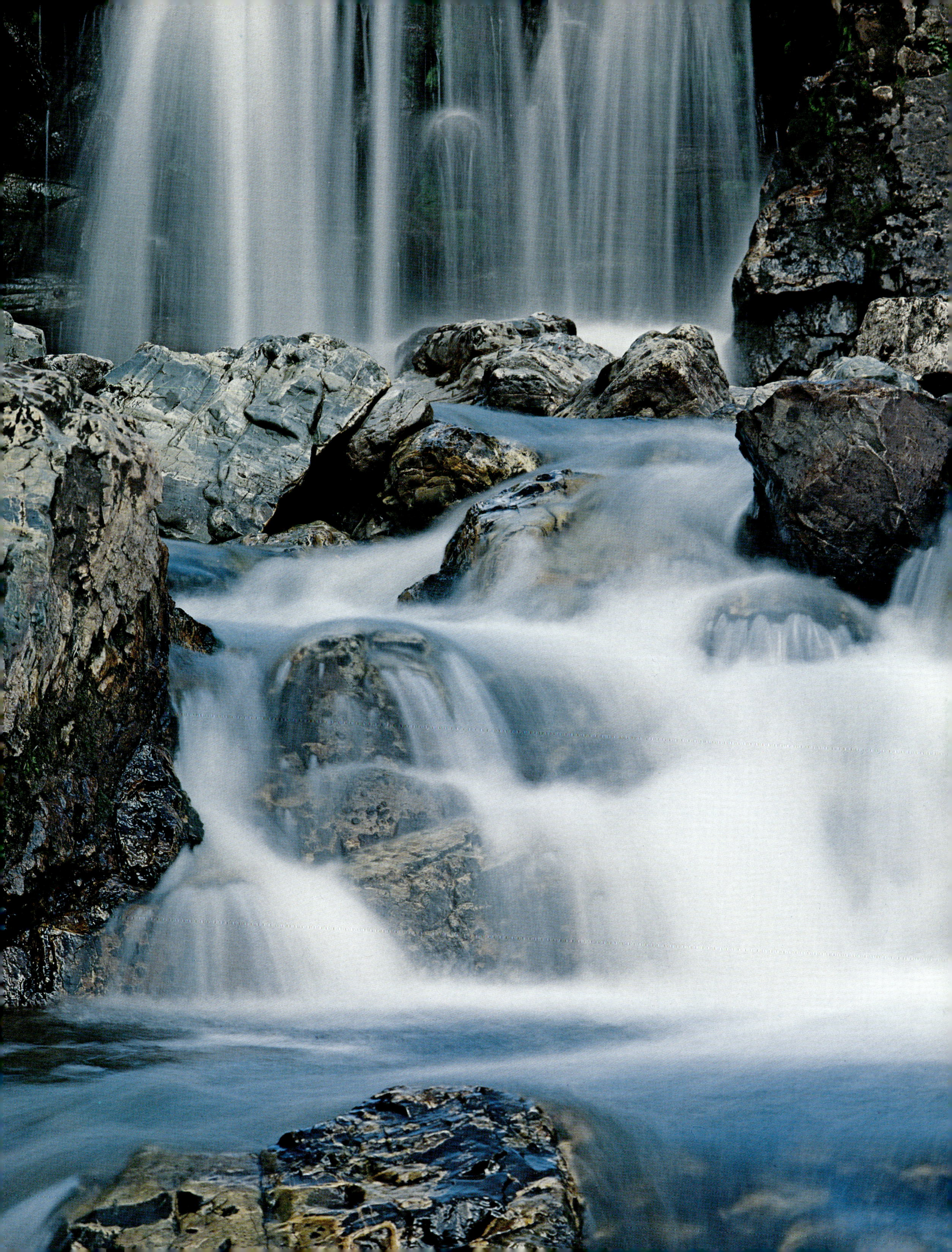

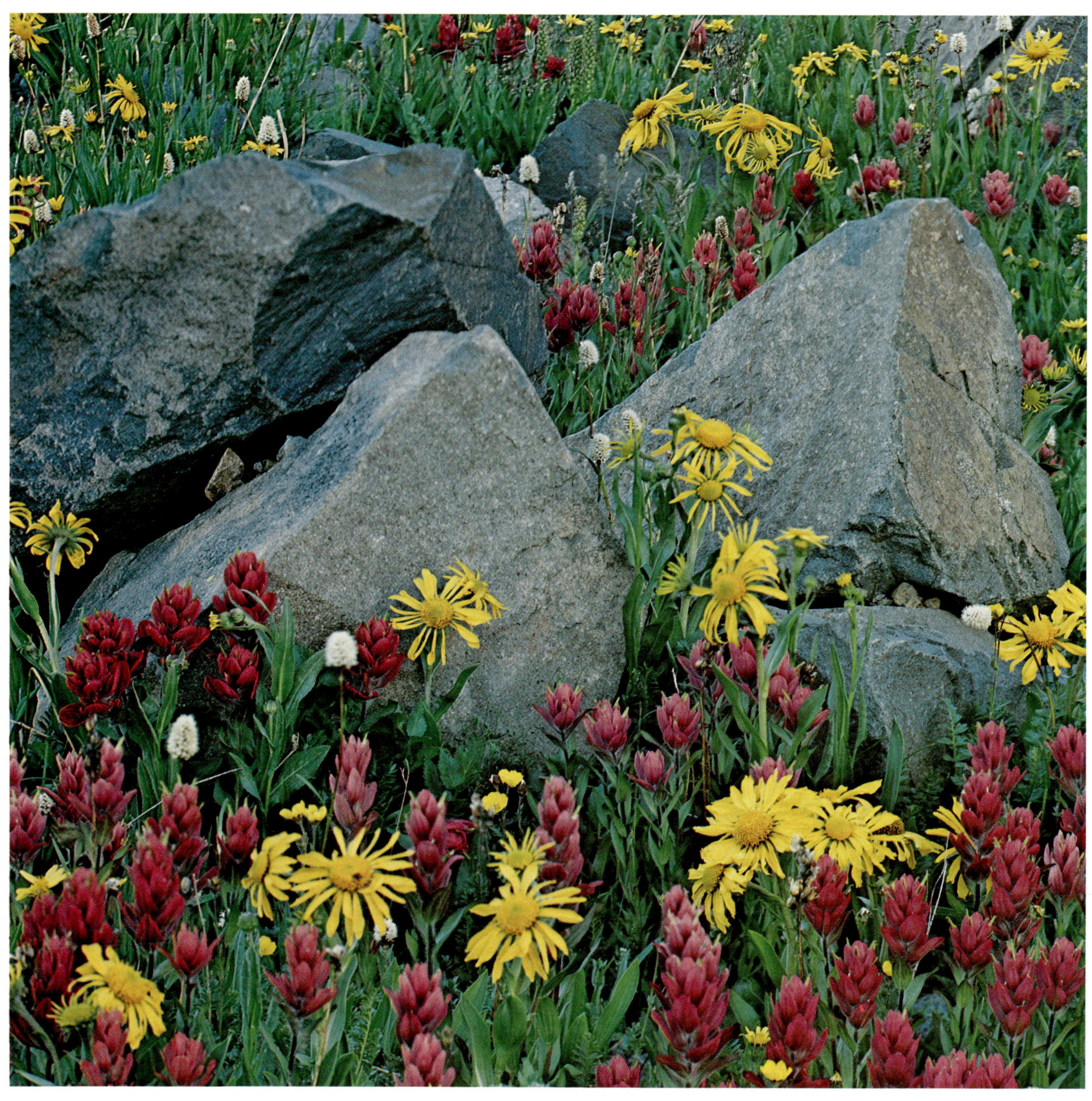

▲ In the San Juan Mountains, Yankee Boy Basin hosts paintbrush, composite, buttercup, and bistort.
► Red Rock Lake, below Indian Peaks in the Front Range, appears placid.

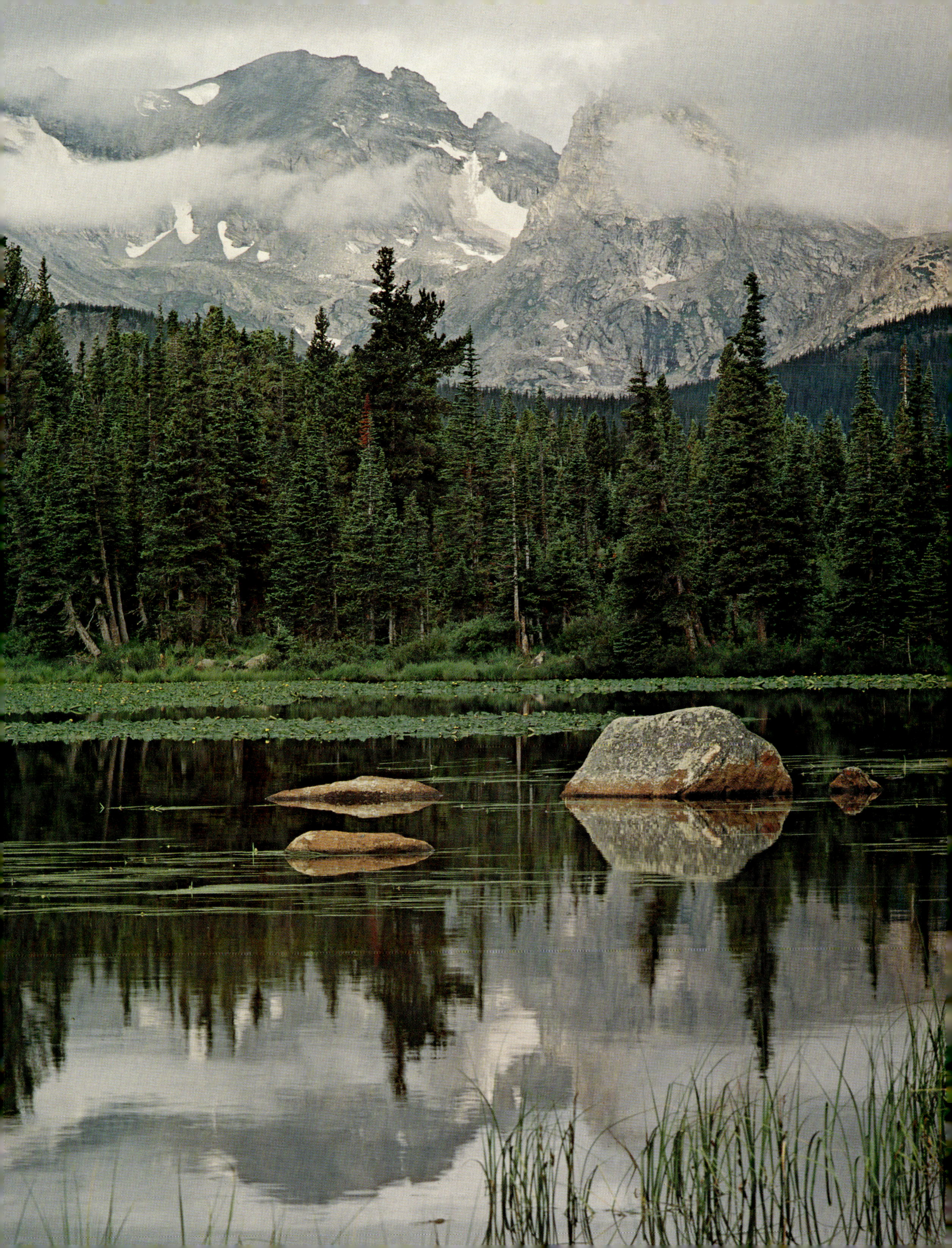

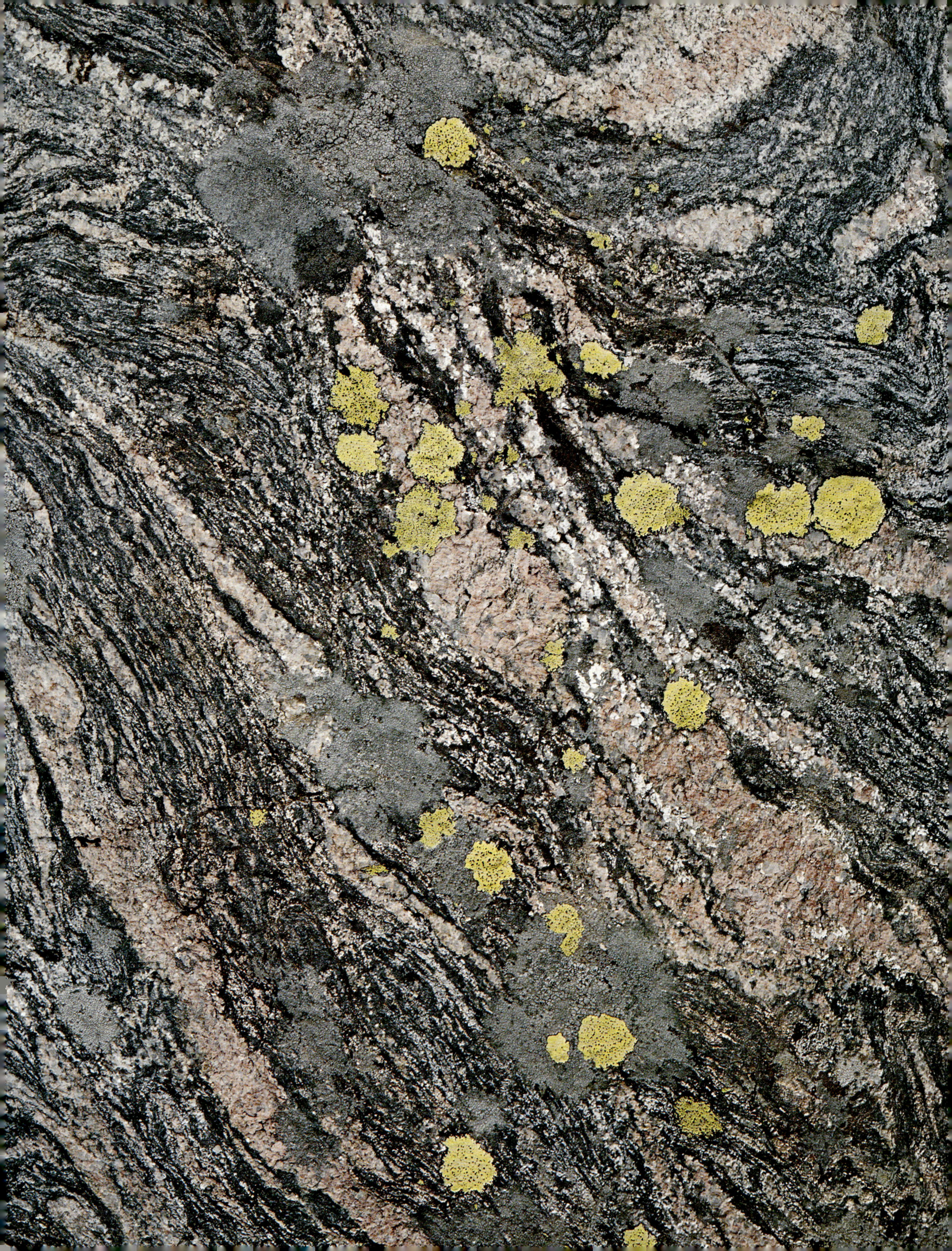

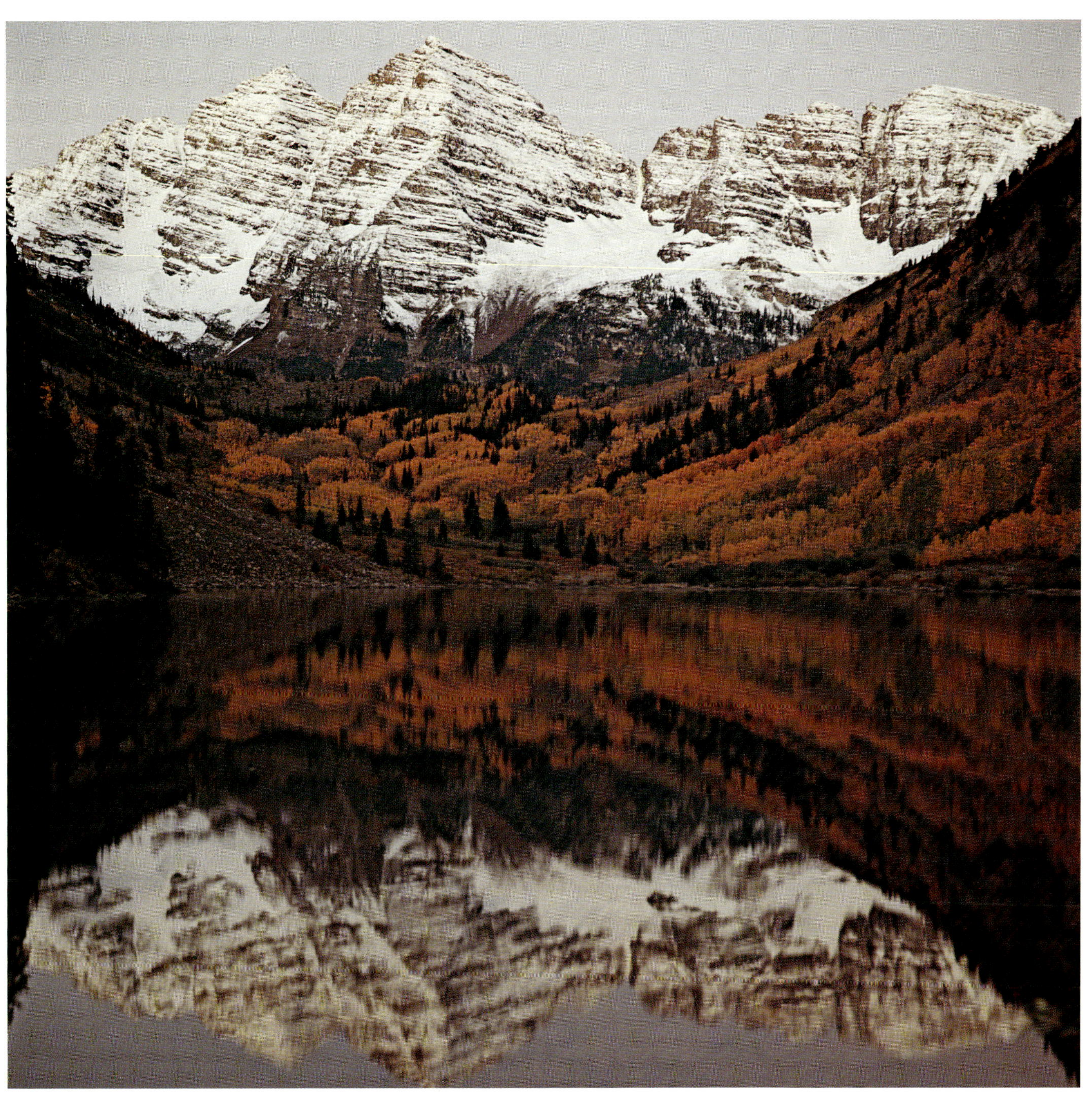

◄ Lichen paints the pink granite façade of Notch Mountain.
▲ Near Aspen, Maroon Lake reflects Maroon Bells' sedimentary lines of age.

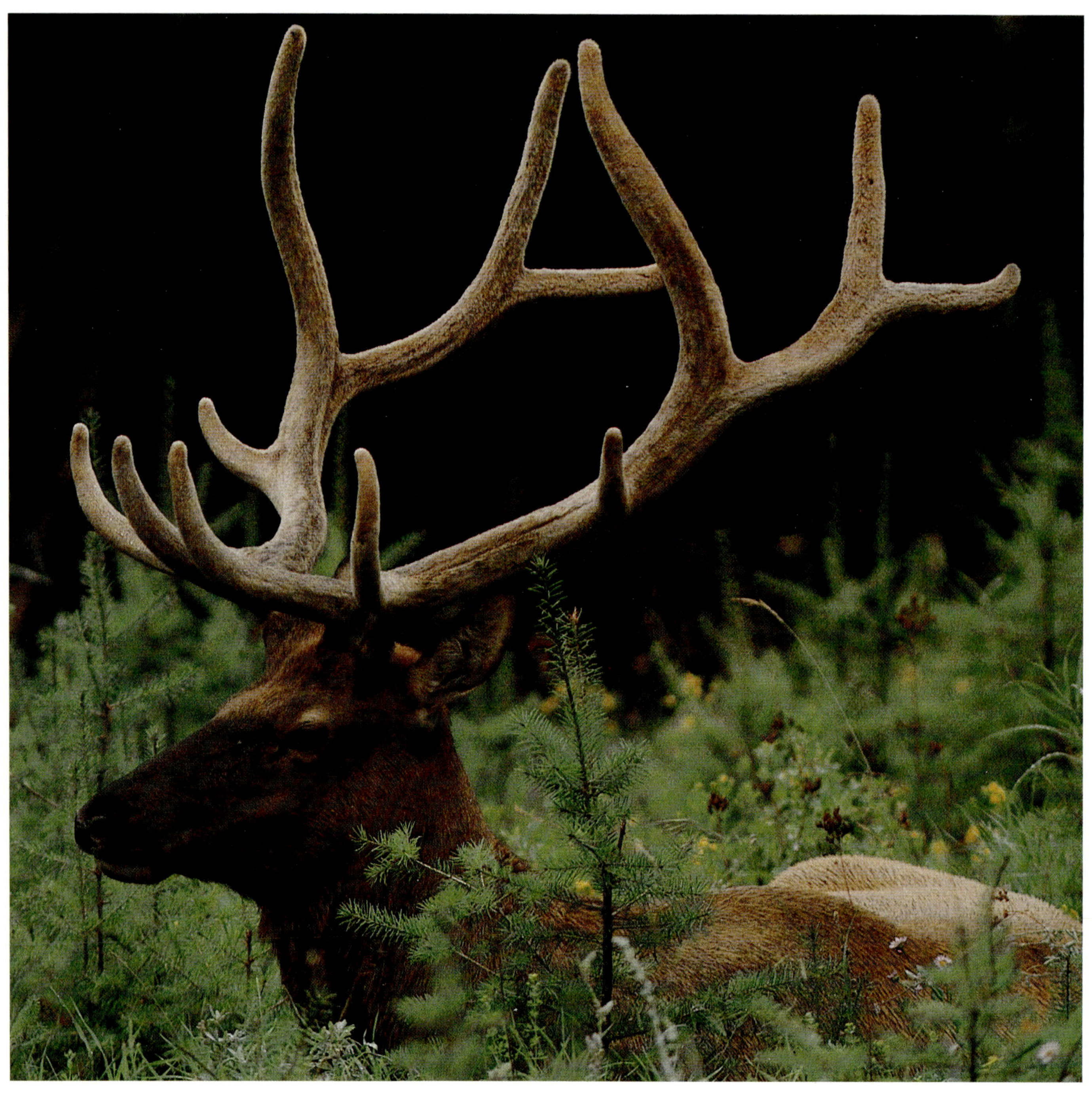

▲ A bull elk, also known by the Algonquian name of *wapiti,* rests in the shade.
► Bristlecone pine, the oldest known living things, bend to the prevailing winds on the slopes of Mosquito Range.

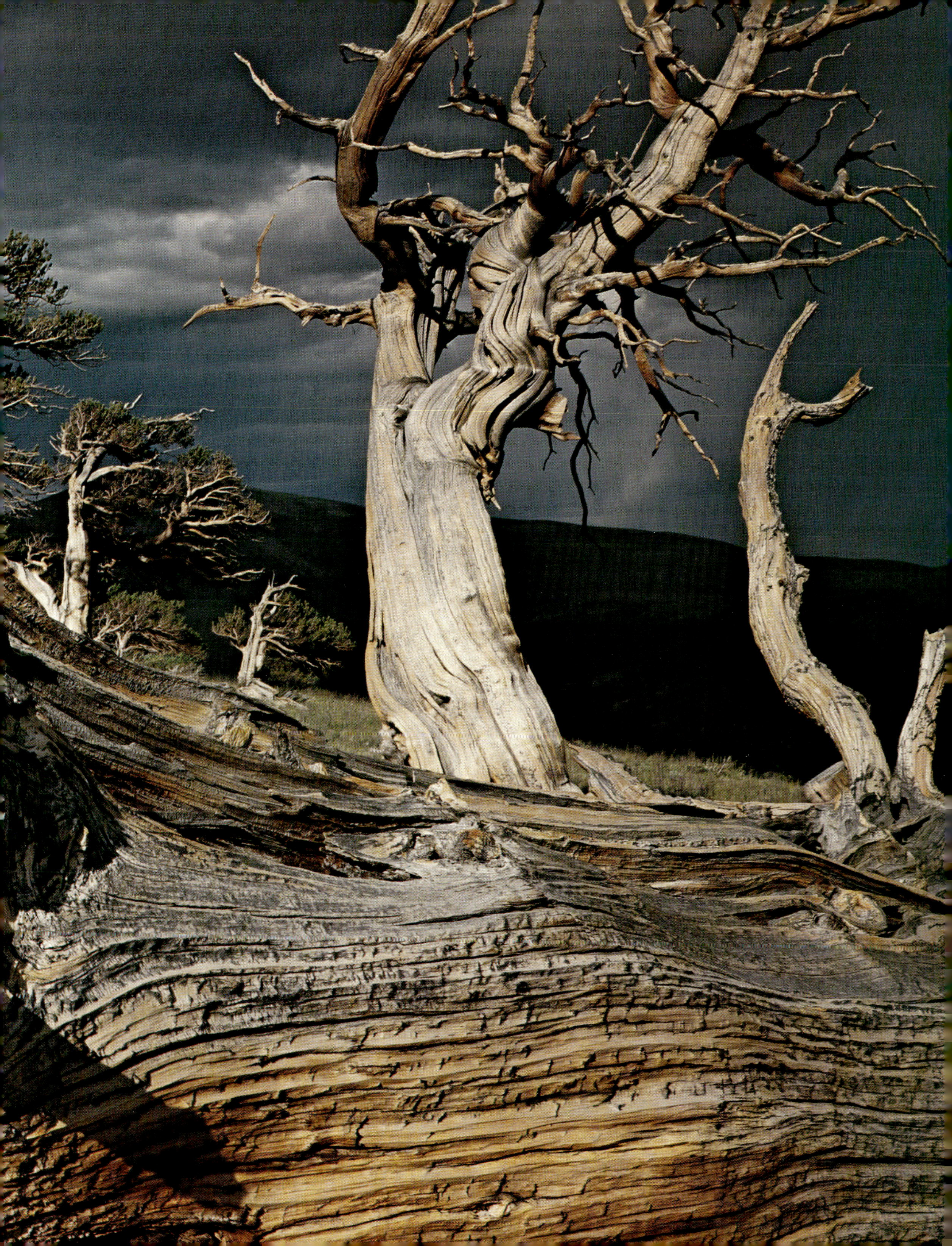

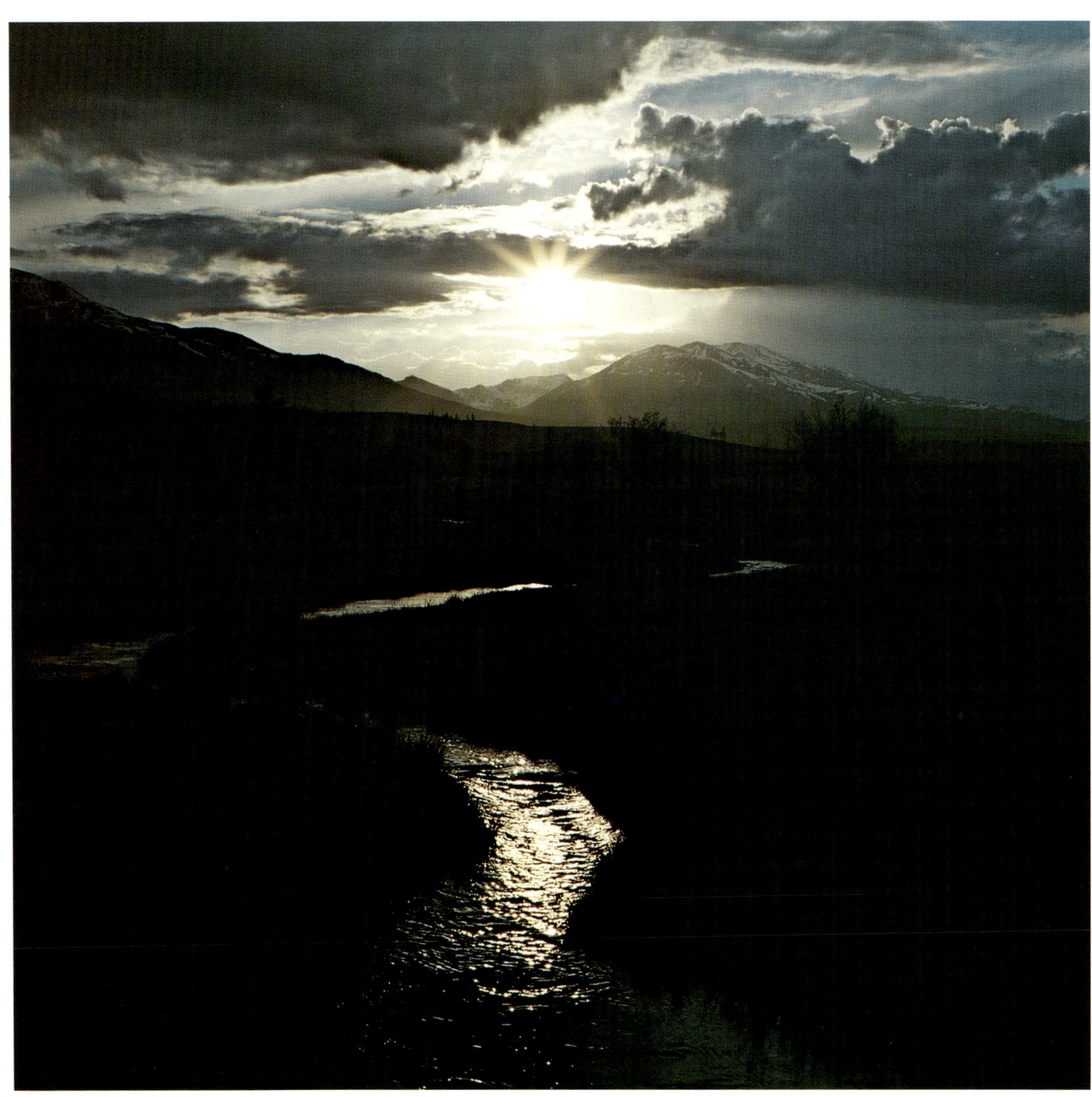

▲ Sun breaks through clouds above Arkansas River Valley near the two-mile-high mining town of Leadville.
► In Rocky Mountain National Park, sunrise flushes peaks along the Continental Divide above Sprague Lake.
► ► Roaring Fork River, fed by Hunter and Castle creeks, flows around multi-hued cobbles near Aspen.

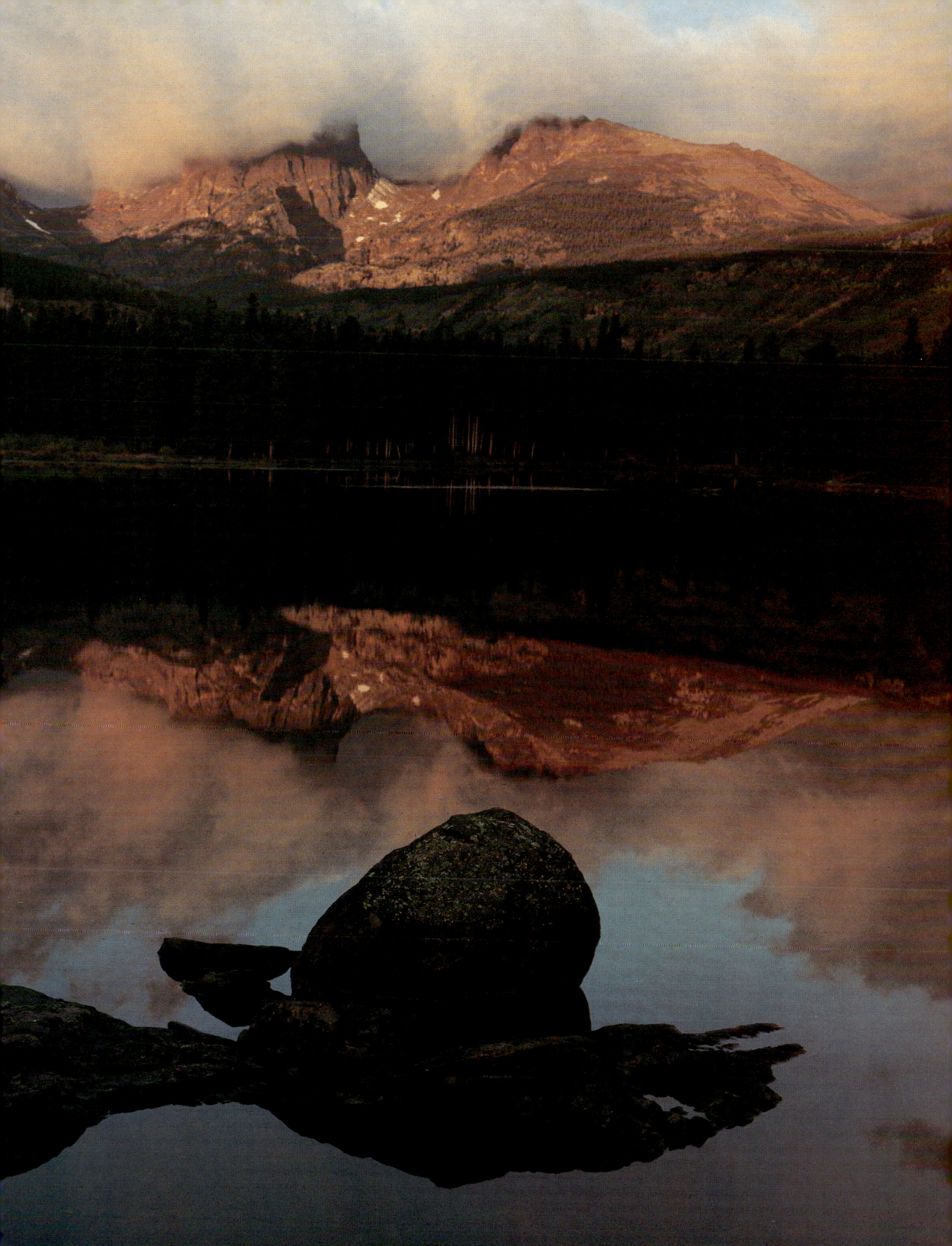

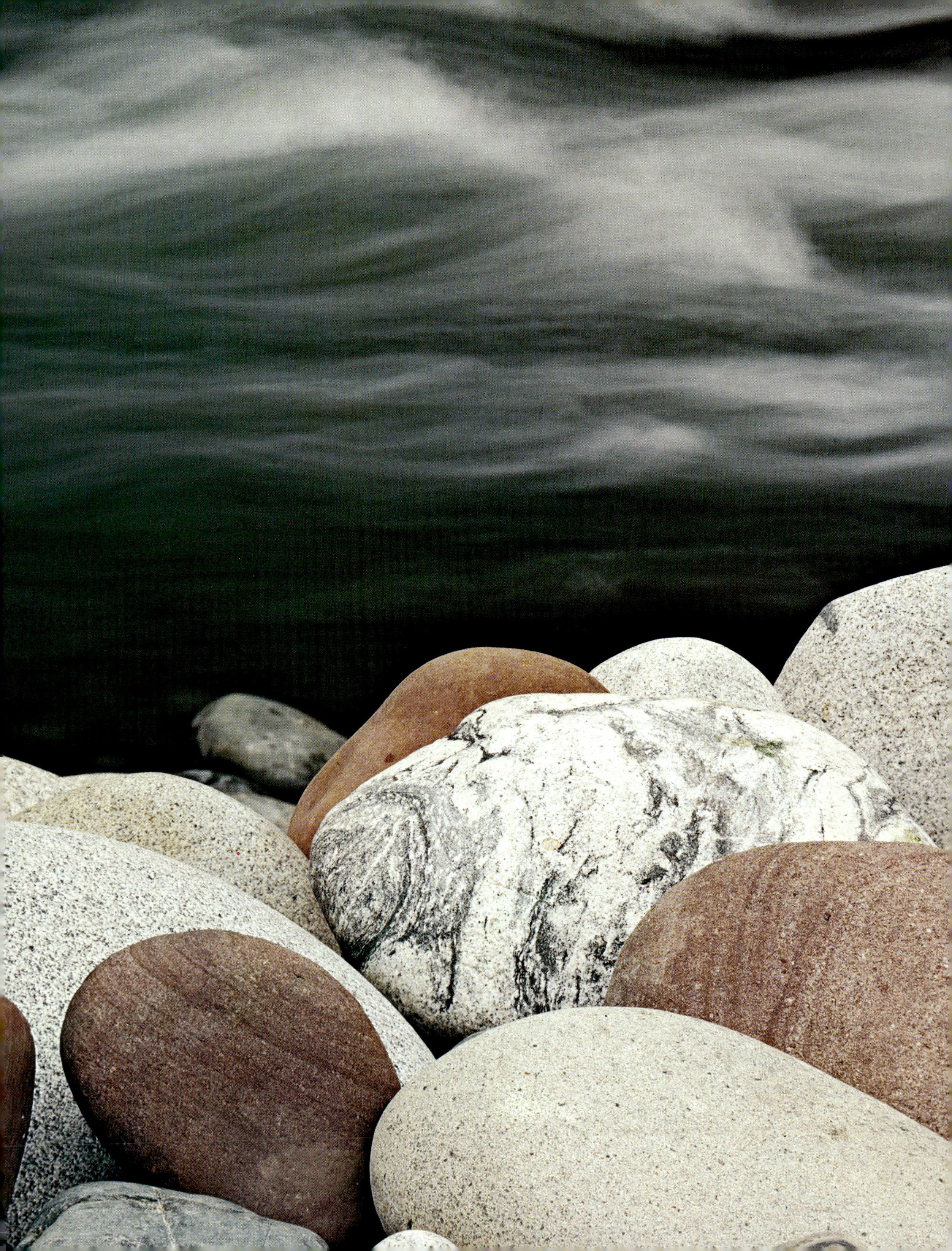

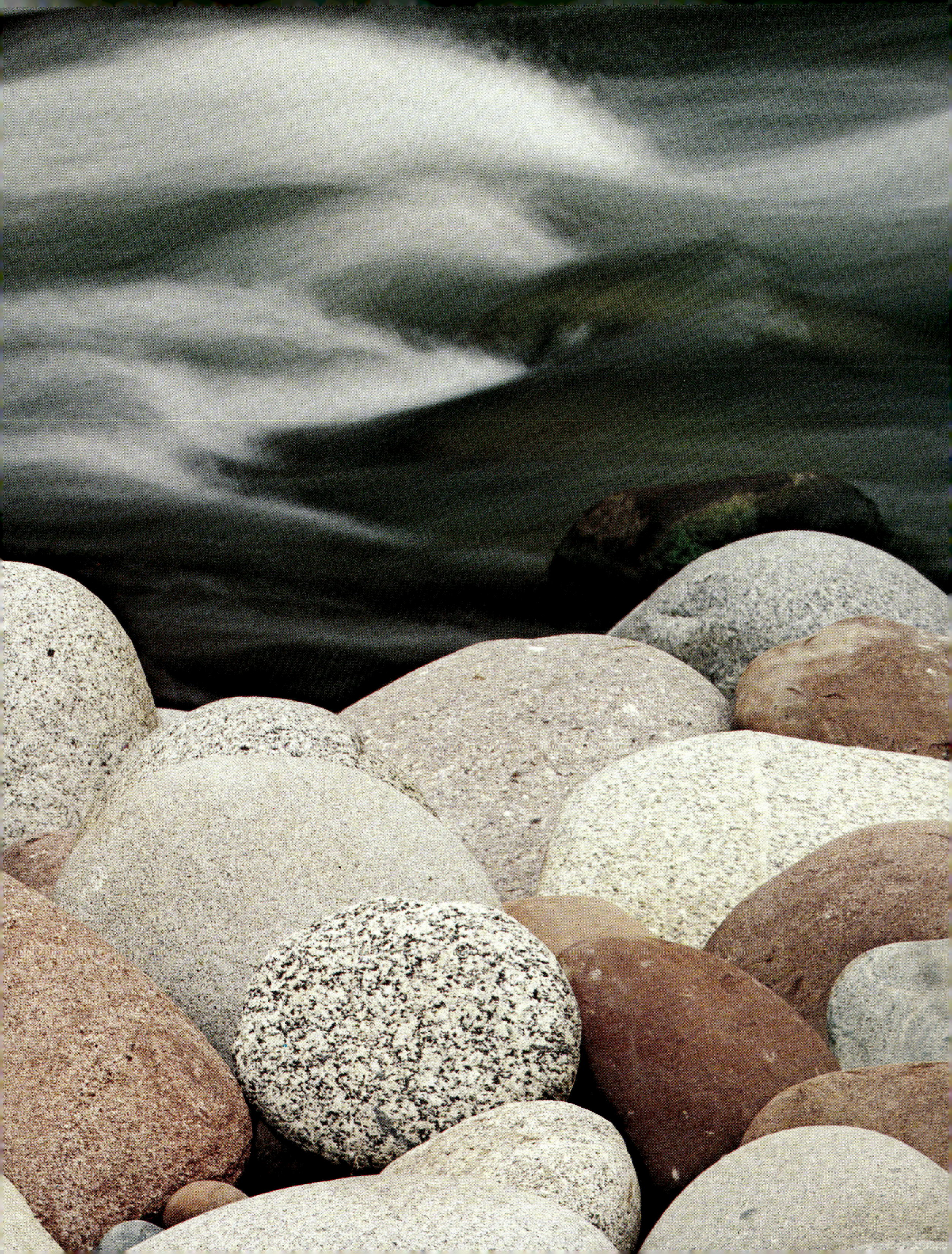

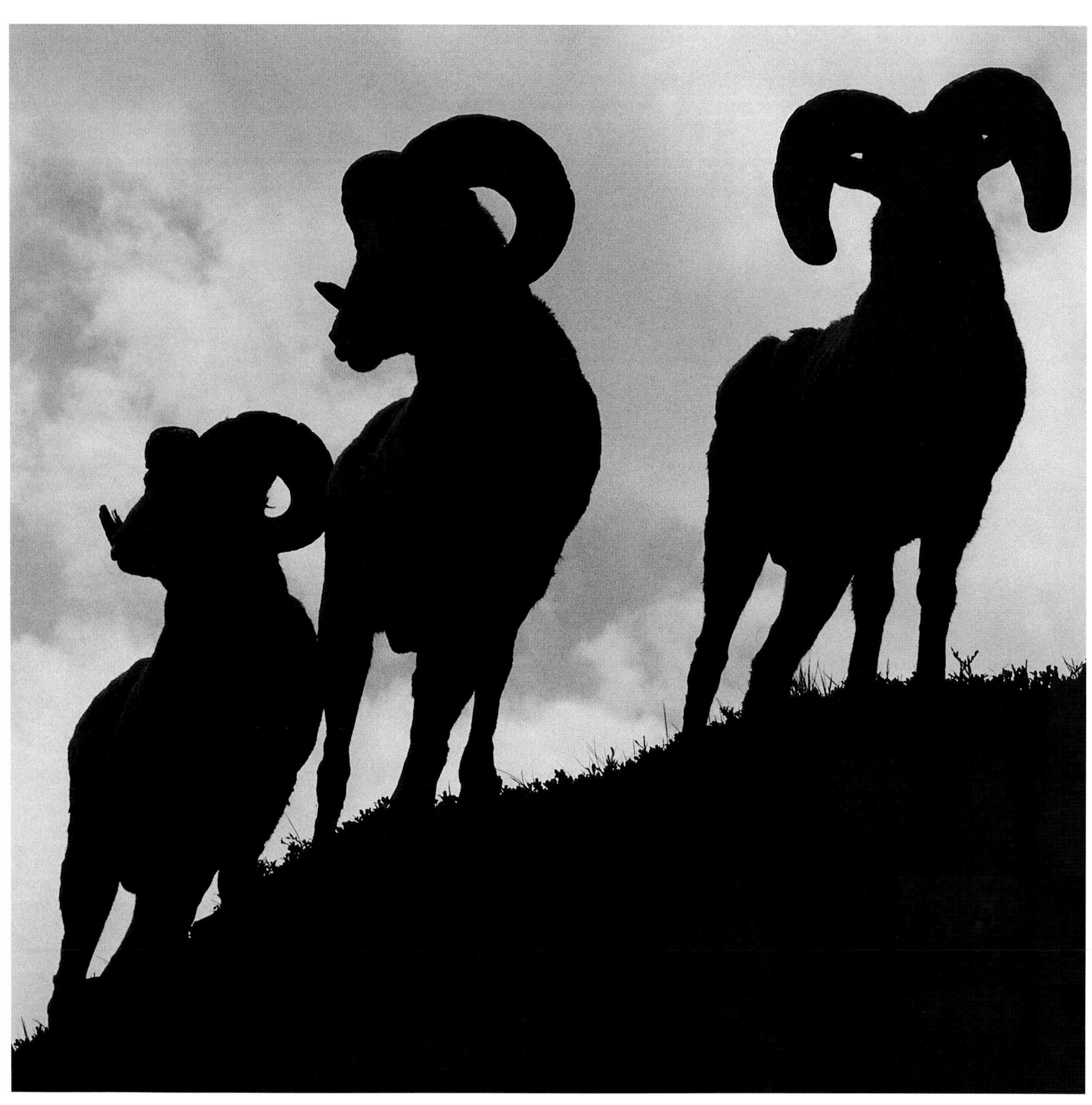

▲ Wary Rocky Mountain bighorn sheep rams browse subalpine slopes in spring.
► In the Sangre de Cristo Range, Crestone Peak, at 14,294 feet, backdrops a lichen-spattered rock.

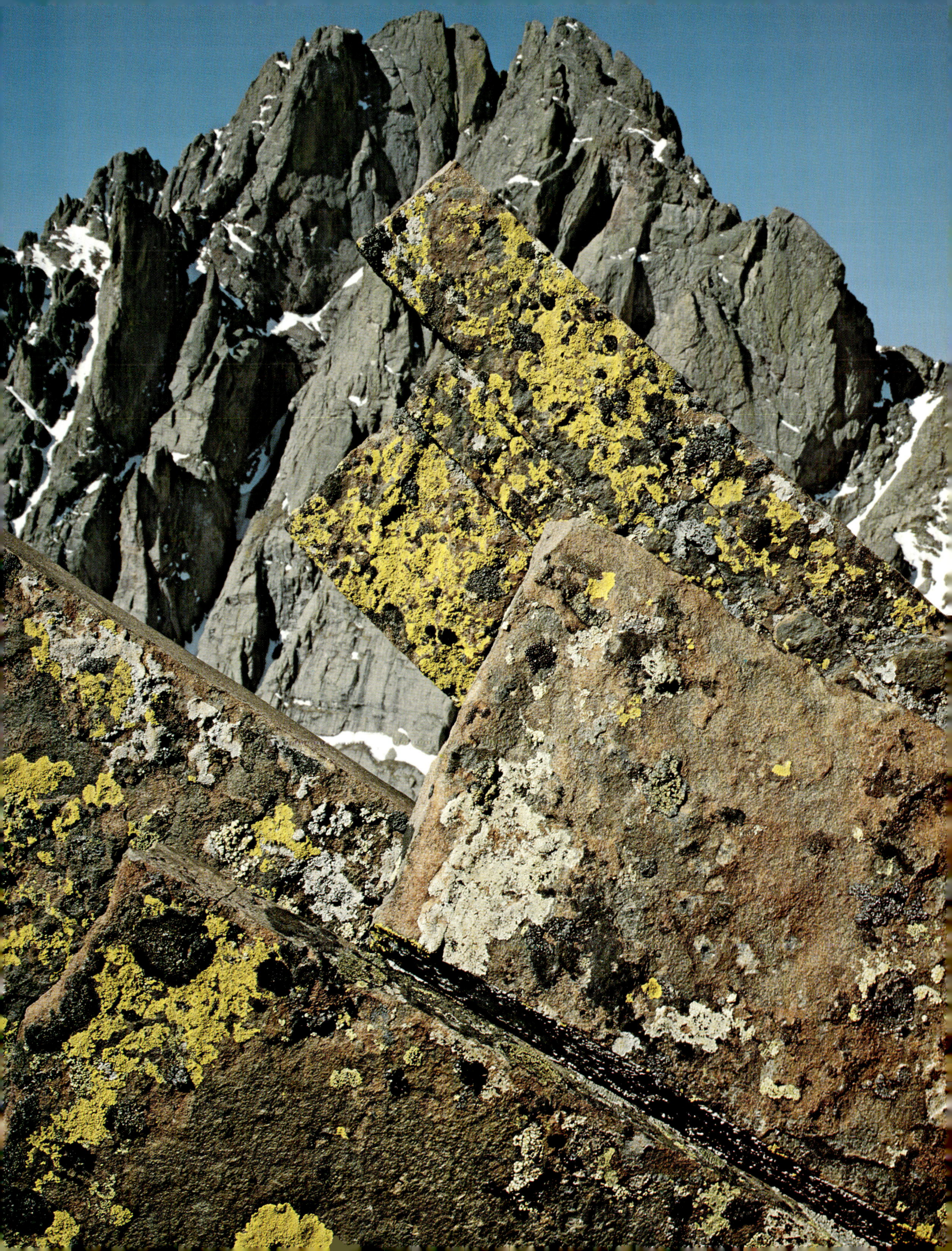

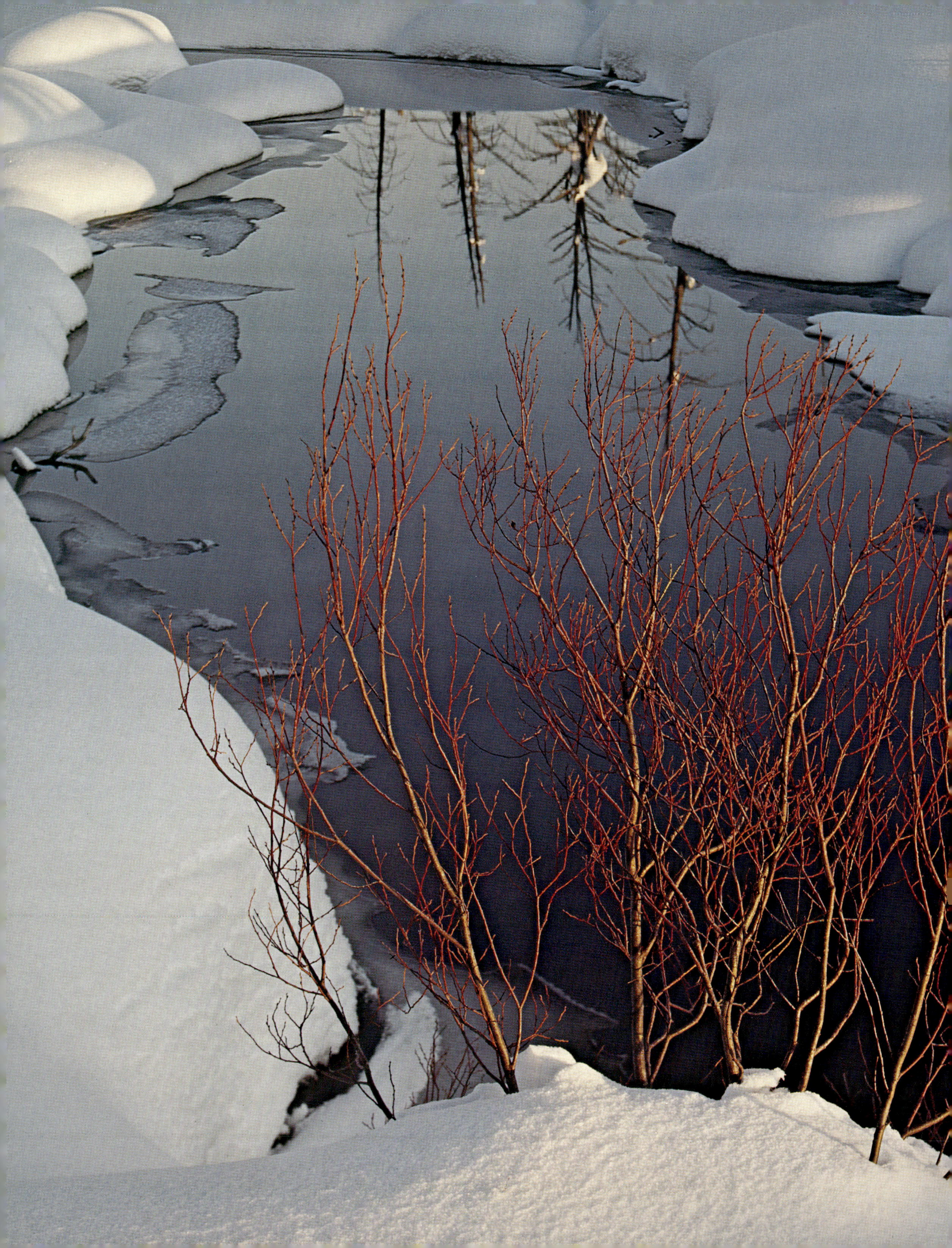

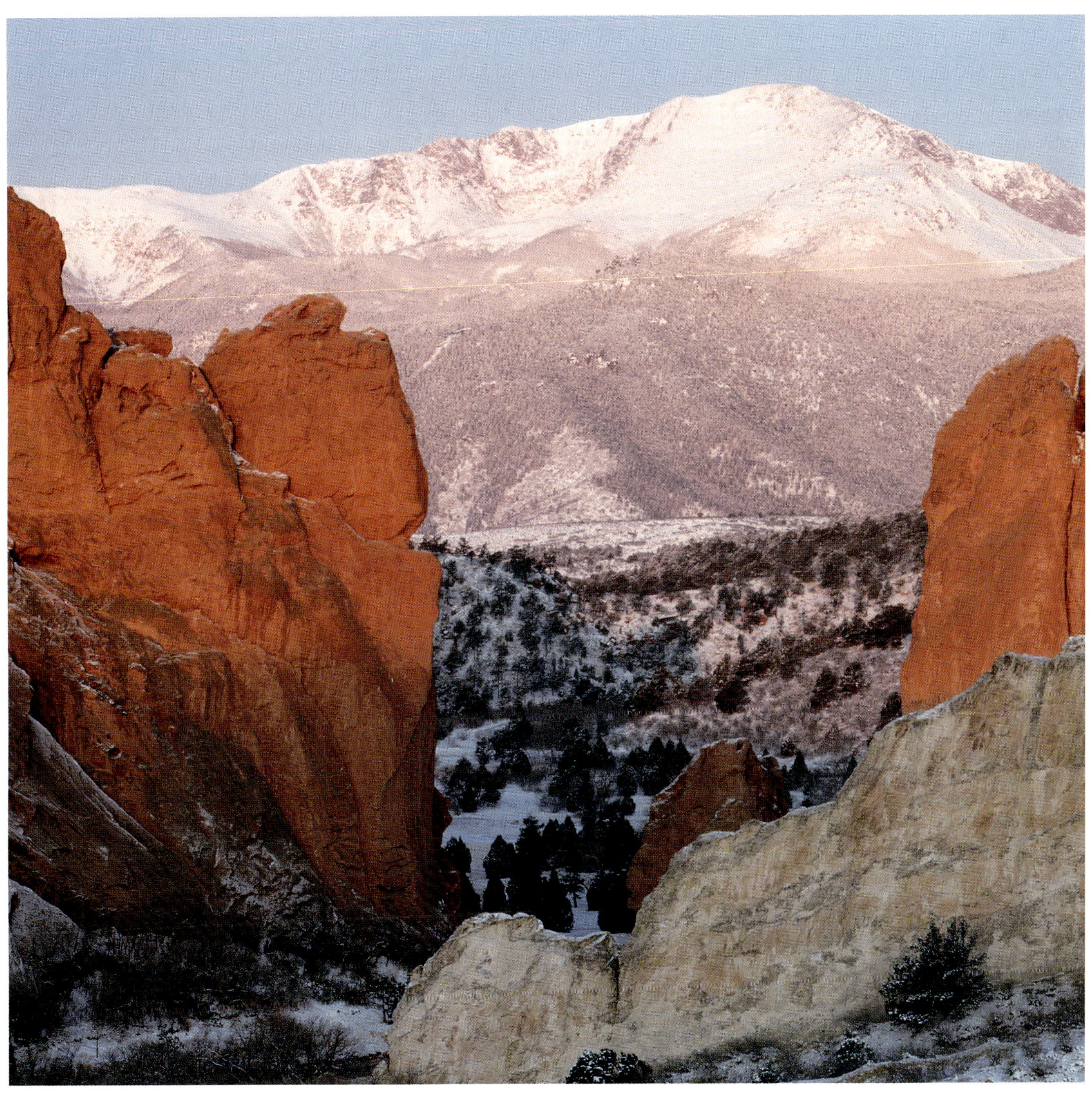

◄ The silent blows of winter lock up stream water for an eight-month season in the Arkansas River Valley.
▲ High above Garden of the Gods, Pikes Peak (14,110 feet) was sighted but not climbed by explorer Zebulon Pike.

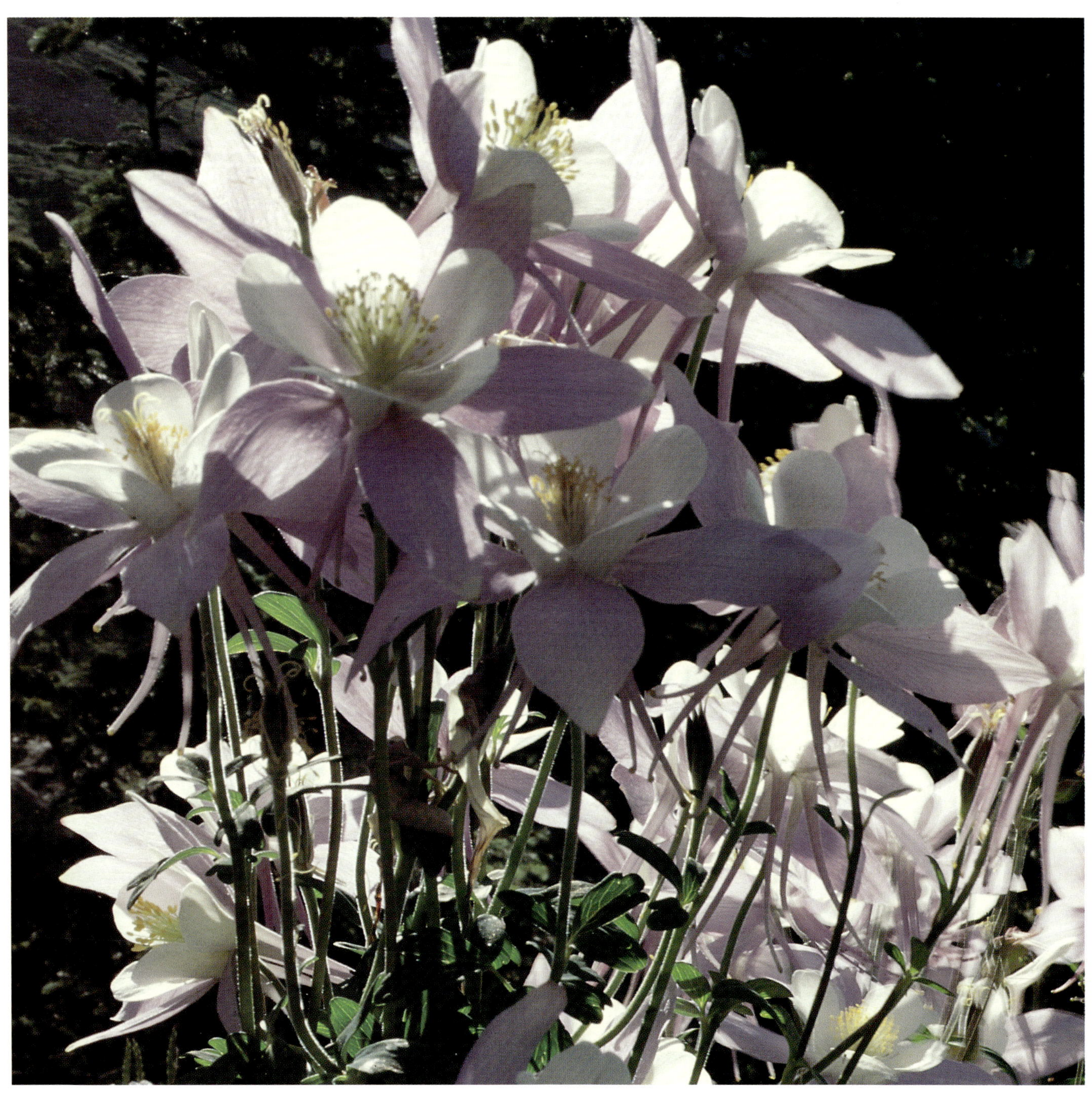

▲ Blue columbine flourishes at timberline in Yankee Boy Basin above Ouray.

COLORADO
by David Sumner

I. DISCOVERIES

Toward evening I was struck with a peculiar tint in the shadow of a cloud along the horizon to the west. After half an hour's study, I pronounced it to be a mountain—and, of course, Pikes Peak. As the clouds dissolved, the outline of a snowy peak came out sharp and clear.

—Baynard Taylor, *Colorado: A Summer Trip* (1867)

My first experience of Colorado came from the hothouse cab of a twenty-foot U-Haul van truck rolling west in fit mythic style. Next to me, on the floor, panting, lay my dog, and packed in behind was all I owned, including a small British sports car. That was in August, a scorcher of a day that began in a motel in Kearney, Nebraska.

Toward noon I passed the Big Springs exit, swung southwest on what is now I-76, and, in a few miles, arrived. "Welcome to Colorful Colorado," said the wooden sign. "Elevation 3,417," read a second. All around, the land was a tawny, monochrome brown, largely level. I eased off the accelerator, thinking I ought to stop and celebrate, but the impulse passed. Like other modern immigrants, I came to Colorado "to be in the mountains." No matter that I knew only vaguely what I meant by the phrase. This wasn't it.

On I drove. More brown landscape, growing slowly rougher, more broken, with ranks of dust-green cottonwoods along the South Platte River. The elevation crept past 4,000 feet, gaining an average of ten feet a mile. Above Brighton, 150 miles into Colorado, the mountains finally appeared. The sun was dropping in the west, and stacks of summer thunderheads piled above the horizon so that at first I could not tell what I was seeing—could not separate the outline of peaks from the light-charged mass.

I did not know exactly what to expect, but what I saw sufficed. The mountains did not loom up; they were not foreboding, not even imposing—simply distant and fine, as images often are when they emerge from uncertainty. I studied outlines to distinguish which were moving and which were not, then separated foothill from peak. I drove on, checking the mountains, watching them grow, become darker, sharper, and more distinct in the afternoon glare.

As a child I had collected stamps, Viewmaster reels, and back issues of *National Geographic*. I gained pictures not only of Yellowstone, Yosemite, Grand Canyon, and Bryce, but also of Rocky Mountain and Mesa Verde in Colorado.

Other images of the state emerged later. A friend went skiing at Aspen. Someone else rode through Colorado on the diesel Zephyr and enjoyed the view from the Vista Dome. One summer, two friends drove from Boston to Breckenridge in an old, converted hearse. Finally, in honor of my first full-time job, I decided to go to Colorado.

Many have arrived in Colorado with images as vague as mine to see what this place was all about. No matter that they knew little at the outset; discovering Colorado has long been part of its allure.

Zebulon Montgomery Pike made the first such discovery of record. In 1806, with a mixed troop of whites and Indians, he headed west from Belle Fontaine, Missouri. Pike was a Lieutenant in the U.S. Army, and the territory that was to become Colorado was a mix of blank space, misconception, mystery, and dream. There were no reliable maps: only sketches and conflicting reports, part rumor, part fact. Thomas Jefferson's "Description of Louisiana," an 1803 account of the territory he had bought for $15 million sight unseen, figured the headwaters of the Missouri, Colorado, and Rio Grande might all conveniently interlock. It noted a "prairie too rich for the growth of trees," and a mountain mass 180 miles by 45 "composed of solid rock salt without any trees or even shrubs on it." Other shadowy information filtered east: a mountain chain dividing Atlantic and Pacific drainages; strange animals—cabrie (pronghorn antelope), brelaw (bighorn sheep), panther, grizzly bear; a volcano on the upper Missouri; a river of brine coming in from the West; a mountain of crystal; mines of silver and gold.

Pike's expedition was a "military reconnaissance," meaning he was to get on good terms with several Indian nations, police "any unlicensed traders," find the sources of the Arkansas and Red rivers, and keep notes on "geographical structures, the natural history, and population of the country through which you may pass." Pike had no experienced guide; neither was he a natural plainsman. His journals show him generally emotionless, factual, and terse. Most days, the party covered between fifteen and twenty-five miles, living largely on buffalo meat and feeling generally "forlorn and dreary" about the endless plains.

In November 1806, the group crossed what is now the Kansas-Colorado line. Next day two horses gave out; the day after, a turkey was shot. Two days later, Pike wrote in his expedition diary: "At two o'clock in the afternoon I thought I could distinguish a mountain to our right, which appeared like a small, blue cloud; viewed it with the spy glass, and was still more confirmed in my conjecture." Half an hour later the party topped a rise and, continued Pike, "with one accord we gave three cheers to the Mexican mountains."

They were seeing the central Rockies; in the end, this ecstatic moment of the 225-day journey mattered more than all the rest. Pike called his mountain "Highest Peak," or "Grand Peak," "the North Mountain," "the Blue Mountain," but did not name it. He made a "meridianal observation" of the peak and got its elevation at 18,581 feet, a magnificent height in any day, and only 4,471 in excess of its present measure. Toward Thanksgiving, with a surgeon and two privates, he set out to climb his mountain, but the scale of the landscape in the clear air confounded him. Instead of an expected three-day hike to the summit and back, they were out for five and never got above the high foothills. The great peak was deep in "eternal snows" and, wrote Pike, "I believe no human being could have ascended to its pinnacle." Under the conditions, he was surely right. When they turned back, the four were "middle deep" in snow, dressed in "light overalls," with "no stockings," and also "ill provided . . . hungry, thirsty and extremely sore."

The rest of Pike's journey—though a confused, grueling feat—is a footnote. The party probed the Royal Gorge of the Arkansas, floundered through snow into the mountains, got lost, turned around, ended up back at the gorge, pushed into the mountains again, crossed two ranges, dropped into an eight-thousand-foot desert valley, retreated to the foothills of a third range, and holed up. Troops of New Spain, garrisoned in New Mexico, caught up with Pike and his men and marched them to Santa Fe for trespassing on foreign soil.

No government expedition would return to Colorado until Long's in 1820, and none would explore so much until Fremont and Gunnison came along in 1848 and 1853, over a generation later. But symbolically, no episode would mean more to Colorado than Pike's encounter with his peak. In the national eye, his feat replaced *terra incognita* with a single image—something to be proud of, able to match the capacity for wonder. Returning east, Pike published his account: *A Journal of a Voyage to the Sources of the Arkansas*. At last, Colorado had its first press release.

Others moved into the mountains—getting a precise, intricate fix on the country. As a group they were superbly bright and able, but they were not learned; they made no maps, put little in writing. Mountain men, or fur trappers, focused on one zone of the mountains: beaver habitat. Since beavers lived everywhere, there was food and water to dam; mountain men explored every major creek and river drainage in the state from above timberline down to the plains. The mountain man era spanned from 1811 to 1840.

Colorado was great trapping country, but the fur trade never centered there. Colorado's chain of large, central mountain valleys—North Park, Middle Park, South Park— were choice trapping grounds. The Arkansas, the South Platte, the Gunnison, the Grand (now the Colorado) also yielded furs, as did many smaller streams dropping east onto the plains. New place names appeared—Pikes Peak, Cache le Poudre, Bayou Salado. A few forts showed up (St. Vrain, Davy Crockett, Bent's), becoming Colorado's first permanent outposts.

Most mountain men came from Kentucky and Tennessee. To many people, they seemed a bunch of drop-outs, outcasts

adventuring out in no man's land. None got rich trapping, few were solvent, and fewer cared. The nomadic life and open space suited them. That was enough.

What this crew added to the discovery of Colorado is not as clear as it might seem. They did explore new country, named landmarks, and straightened out maps of the West. But they made no symbolic discovery like Pike, and they left no major accounts of their wanderings. Instead, they sharpened the nation's generic image of mountain wilderness and what it exacted from those who chose to work it for pelts. Western mountains were vast, intricate, and demanding— not one range but a complex of many; not just glistening peaks, but also parks, holes, passes, gorges, basins, creeks, lakes. The climate could be dangerous; likewise the up-and-down terrain, Indians, "griz," loneliness, and space. Food was not always available. Trapping was specialized, back-breaking labor, requiring constant alertness and fine skill. If it was also high adventure, no matter; the rest of America was not much interested in so much risk for so little reward. There was no great rush west to trap beaver.

Colorado was a loner's place, without gaudy claims, until its gold rush began in the late 1850s with rumbles in towns like Kansas City, St. Louis, Omaha, and Fort Leavenworth. The California rush had occurred almost a decade earlier; the association of mountains and sudden wealth had passed into folklore; a recession was in progress (low wages, high prices); the nation was in a vulnerable, frustrated mood, ready to jump. From the far edge of the plains in what was then Kansas Territory, right at the base of the Rocky Mountains, stories of gold began trickling back east. True, gold had been rumored for years in "the Pikes Peak Country," but never like this.

The summer of 1858 was the year of Colorado's first mass discovery. Against the mountains, Denver City and Auraria sprang up on opposite banks of Cherry Creek, but gold appeared only in random dribs and drabs. Then, in 1859, a true strike occurred. John Gregory was a marginally literate Georgian who had picked up on the 1858 rumors; having nothing better to do, he wintered in Colorado and, just as deeper snows were melting off the mid-elevation mountains west of Denver, he found gold-bearing quartz. Lingering drifts blocked Gregory's return to Denver for a week, but when he bobbed up with $80 in gold in a vial, the excitement was on, and news quickly rippled back east.

William Hawkins Hedges was a farmer, surveyor, and engineer working at the time in Sidney, Iowa. Word of the Gregory Diggins magnetized him. "Living near the edge of civilization," he wrote in *Pikes Peak or . . . Busted!*, "with a young man's undecided future before me, I fell an easy victim to the prevailing gold fever, and with a young friend named Charley Dewey, determined on trying for a fortune in the Golden West." The tone is matter-of-fact, the notion fabulous. "Everyone was doing it," he seems to say. "Something to try so why shouldn't I?"

Hedge's journey west differs from that of explorers and mountain men, not only because he traveled with an ox-drawn wagon, but also because it was a social event. A "movement" was in progress rather than an isolated episode or a small-scale caravan. At the height of the fur era, the number of trappers working the streams of the Rockies was six hundred. On any given day in June 1859, some forty thousand gold seekers crossed the plains to Denver.

A complete, four-man wagon outfit (including three yoke of oxen, tools, provisions, and necessary sundries) weighed 3,002 pounds and cost $614.35. To the list of basics the *New Illustrated Miner's Hand Book and Guide to Pike's Peak* (St. Louis, 1859) added $54.50 in luxuries, including twelve cans of oysters, four cans of peaches, twenty-seven pounds of chewing tobacco, and a half barrel of bourbon. Going west no longer had to be pure roughin' it either.

Hedges made no note of the prairie landscape save that it seemed largely "sand, cactus and Prairie Dog towns." Unlike Pike and many earlier travelers, his sighting of the mountains fails to signal the end of the long plains journey. His elation comes later. "A mile or so further and from a little rise in the prairie," he wrote of a moment on a long night march under a full moon, "we looked down on a host of twinkling lights that said Denver lie before us." The miner discovered, not the wonder of mountains, but civilization—the familiar once again—and the gateway to the goldfields.

Hedges and Dewey "were desirous of getting to the place where the nuggets could be gathered in most easily and quickly"—as if gold were a crop to be picked at will. The two were not explorers; their driving impulse was not yearning for the unknown, but simple desire. "No other place I was ever in," wrote Hedges, "was so confusing as to distance and direction, as among those peaks, ridges and valleys." They went to Tarryall town in South Park because of "exciting reports of discoveries of Fabulous Richness." They worked hard, endured privation, found nothing, and two months later pulled up stakes and left—homesick and "utterly 'Busted.'" By nature, a mining boom brings to an area many people who are just passing through.

Mining brought civilization to Colorado; from 1859 to the early 1890s, discovering the state meant landing in a supply center like Denver, or in one of the hundreds of mountain camps: Silverton, Silver Cliff, Telluride, Tincup, Tomboy, Bonanza, Eureka, Royal Flush, Hessie, Buckskin Joe. With rare exceptions, these settlements appeared and mushroomed spontaneously. In April 1860, Tarryall was an uninhabited, open slope on the edge of South Park. Two months later, it counted six groceries, a drug store, a whole-sale provision store, a justice of the peace, a meat market, a hotel, three boarding houses, two doctors, a lawyer, a recorder's office, two blacksmith shops, five stock ranches, thirty-five buildings completed, thirty going up. Tarryall happened too fast for a census; government and law were typically *ad hoc.* In all, Tarryall's mines produced some $2 million in gold; by 1875, they had played out, and the town was vacant. Most Colorado camps pursued this sequence. As with individuals like Hedges, many more mine towns busted than made it.

Today, some of these failures remain as ghost towns. Avalanche, gale, snow, sun, and wind have reduced many more to shattered, overgrown shards—a foundation here, a snarl of rusted metal there, a shack of dry-rotting boards somewhere else. This is the forgotten part of Colorado, the other side of the fantasy, feverish pace, hoopla, boosterism, and hope that lured people west and built upstart towns overnight. Weathered, windowless husks of buildings are evidence of defeat, and also of an impulse so profligate it could build whole towns and discard them at will.

A few lasted, along with the supply centers that served them, and the two dovetailed into the state's first settlement pattern. The last and richest Colorado mine camp to boom and persist was Cripple Creek in the hills behind Pikes Peak, a result of random prospecting in what had been cattle country. That was in 1892. By then, much of the blank space on the state maps was well filled in, replaced by a network of dots and connecting lines that denoted towns, wagon routes, and railroads—both narrow and standard gauge.

By 1900, Colorado was largely coterminus with mining in the national eye. Agriculture—farming and ranching—was the state's other activity of consequence, but its ethos was quieter, steadier, more spread out. For a few, mining offered a way of life no less alluring than gold; but for most, it was something to do and get over with, hopefully rich.

The farmer and rancher were different. They, too, played against steep odds. Little water was the toughest handicap; irrigation, an untried technology. The short growing season, shallow soils, bad storms, and predators were in there too. But if you avoided too many bad years in a row, you could achieve a long-term living and pride to go with it.

The coming of the rancher and farmer helped stabilize the boom-or-bust uncertainty of the miners' Colorado. To head west for 160 acres under the Homestead Act was a firmer commitment than striking out after gold. More often than not, the rancher arrived with a family. He was looking not for sudden riches, but rather for a place to settle and sink roots. He figured on staying.

Along the White River and Piceance Creek in western Colorado, settlement began in the 1880s. Most new arrivals were refuges from fading boom camps, taking a second chance in the state. They discovered in ranching an often lonely, resilient life; their accounts are characteristically terse and direct, with little of a miner's soaring expectation.

"At the homestead," recalled a White River resident who went back to 1887, "we had two little log cabins with a wagon shed in between and that's where I was born."

"In them days our meat was deer," adds another old-timer. "We raised all our potatoes and milked one or two cows. Just enough to have milk and cream. The kind of cows we milked were just anything we could manage to get tied up and milked."

Other memories recall more of the ranchers' Colorado.

"When I was growing up our entertainment was horseback riding, skating, dancing, and eating. . . ."

"My mother made all of our clothing. I never wore any boughten clothes until I was about 14."

"They used to paper the kitchen with newspaper. Dad would stand around and read it, so they papered it upside down. He spent too many hours reading the walls."

"We cut cedar posts on these ridges back here. We all helped build fence. They used to put my little sister down in the first post hole so they didn't have to chase her while they worked."

"Wind really blew up there. It blew snow in through the shingles and my husband kept a shovel in the house so we could scoop the snow out in the mornings when we got up."

Agriculture in Colorado caused no booming land rush, only small, brief scrambles stirred by accounts of fifteen-pound turnips, thirty-five-pound cabbages, two-foot-long beets, wheat growing at eighty bushels per acre. Farmers and ranchers settled into the low-elevation open space wherever there was water: the eastern plains, the protected parks and valleys in the mountains, some of the basins and table lands over toward Utah. Unlike mining, Colorado agriculture brought no surge of national attention. Like fur trapping, the work was too hard, the rewards unlikely to liberate one for life. People came to ranch and farm in Colorado because they figured they might get ahead, put a little space around them to call their own.

Finally, people also came to Colorado because they found it beautiful, bracing, diverse, healthy, exciting, open, and different. Richard Baxter Townshend, freshly graduated from Cambridge, crossed the Atlantic and saw Denver for the first time in 1869. "Only five days earlier," he wrote in his *A Tenderfoot in Colorado*, "I had been sweltering at somewhere between 90 and 100 [degrees] in the shade in the moist, heavy air of Manhattan. Now, 2,000 miles west of there, out on the plains, at an elevation of 5,000 feet above sea level and breathing the dry air of the Great American desert . . . already I felt very much better."

The Briton is a pioneer tourist. Traveling west "in a car of the newly opened Union Pacific Railroad," he grumps about the plains by Julesburg: "a treeless waste of yellowish-brown buffalo grass." But he has no need to sight mountains for a lift. He merely feels the climate, notes its contrast with "the clammy heat in New York," and pronounces himself "very much better." Soon he will feel better yet in "the cool, keen air of the Rocky Mountains."

Ambience was the last major discovery in Colorado. American tourism did not commence in earnest until the 1850s, and both settlement and railroads were prerequisites for the new trade. The tourist perception arrived first with the influx of Eastern journalists assigned to cover the hubbub at the gold camps—observers by trade and boosters by habit. Some gazed around and became giddy, so high-toned reports of Colorado's natural gifts trickled back east along with news of the latest gold excitement.

Both Baynard Taylor's *Colorado: A Summer Trip* (New York, 1867) and Samuel Bowles' *The Switzerland of America* (Springfield, Massachusetts, 1869) were lofty journalistic accounts, appealing blends of fact, superlative, and fantasy. Townshend carried a copy of Bowles as he rolled west: images of Colorado preceding life, a now familiar pattern. The territory and its "atmosphere of elixir," Bowles predicted, would soon become known—nay, fabled—"for rest and recreation, for new and exhilarating scenes, for pure and bracing air, for pleasure and for health." Townshend found the words compelling; they drew him west. Once there, however, reality took over, gradually at first, and held him for eight years. Townshend returned twice thereafter, taking tourism far beyond its usual scope.

Early on, he was euphoric. The headaches he came to cure disappeared. "A very jolly week of it we had," he wrote, "camping in the mountains, feasting on Rocky Mountain trout and grouse." He compared Pikes Peak to Mont Blanc and found its "endless cliffs and gullies of naked granite, all glowing red" the more interesting. The air, Townshend concluded, was the key to "the mountain magic of the Rockies"—to "the amazingly sharp clearness of every detail" it allowed him to see.

A tourist is an explorer born too late—curious, eager to discover, observant, yearning, intent. Thus Townshend. In time, Colorado's exotic glow wore off, and he settled into seeing the land and its people straight. He journeyed back and forth from mountains to plains, from wilderness to town; met people (including three territorial governors), joined a federal commission on a peace mission to the Ute Indians, bought and sold a cattle ranch. He later commanded a wagonload of trade goods to the Jemez pueblo in New Mexico, prospected in Colorado's San Juan Range, hauled beer to mines around Leadville, traded horses, and—on his last visit in 1903—took it easy and photographed.

Townshend was an exception. Colorado Springs, at the foot of Pikes Peak, was the territory's first beneficiary of the tourist perception in its more usual mode. Railroad tycoon William Jackson Palmer, a native of Philadelphia, founded and boosted the town to please his wife in 1871; she rejected his creation in favor of Rhode Island, but it was a class resort many others found to their liking.

Genteel folks—many from Boston, Philadelphia, New York, even England—came to Colorado Springs looking for "Eastern life in a Western environment." In the town's hotels, mansions, gazebos, and salons they drank tea beneath a mountain backdrop. Colorado Springs became "Newport in the Rockies." In 1875, a Dr. Samuel E. Solly concluded that the mineral waters of the nearby Manitou Springs relieved or cured dyspepsia, flatulence, bronchial catarrh, waterbrash, and some twenty other maladies and agues. He published his discoveries, and soon new waves of health seekers joined the Brahmins below Pikes Peak. Manitou Springs soon became the "Saratoga of the West."

From the beginning, Pikes Peak was in on the build-up, a symbol once again. In 1873, the mountain was measured again, this time by Dr. Ferdinand Vandiveer Hayden of the U.S. Geological Survey of the Territories. Hayden, fresh from a landmark charting of the Yellowstone country, was nationally known; the publicity brought to the Colorado Springs area was far more important than the peak's new elevation (14,147, just 37 feet above today's figure). That same year, the mountain gained a horse trail up its flank and a weather station on its summit.

The horse trail made Pikes Peak more easily accessible to tourists, but not accessible enough. In 1889, a carriage road was built to the summit, opening it to four-horse surreys and an entrepreneur of blithe zeal who erected a billboard announcing the arrival of Adam Forepaugh's Circus. Two years later a cog railway went up, inspiration of Zalmon C. Simmons, the mattress king, who wished travelers to have "the greatest comfort technology could provide" on Pikes Peak as well as in bed. For added convenience, the summit auto road was opened in 1915; and for added notoriety, the first car race took place the following year.

The tourist's discovery of Colorado lacks the clarity of the explorer's, the fur trapper's, and the rancher's; it lacks the singleness of the miner's. But being a leisure pursuit, it can get along just fine in a relaxed, heightened haze. Its basic impulse is a desire for something different, a quest for contrast, for diversity. Sometimes its goals are positive (adventure, enrichment, health) and sometimes not (escape from the drab, relief from the crowded, the ugly). Most Colorado tourists do not want too much contrast—enough to connect with a reassuring degree of diversity, but not enough to seem foreign or feel uncomfortable.

Colorado the image and Colorado the reality. Ever since Pike, first the territory (under whatever name) and then the state confronted successive arrivals with the raw fact of a land magnificently endowed, difficult, dry, diverse, open, and rich. Each arrival had a characteristic way of discovering Colorado. The explorers found essentially what they saw.

Fur trappers did likewise, adapted, and made a bare living. Farmers and ranchers faced the land as it was, irrigated, and settled. If any read into Colorado their own highest sense of possibility, the reality of the place quickly brought them down. From out on the plains, Pike's mountain may have seemed momentarily fabulous; from his closest approach in the foothills, it became formidable.

No matter. The facts flowed back east to be winnowed, rearrayed, and enlarged to fit the dreams: nuggets the size of your fist; vegetables and fruits ripening in profusion; "great fountains of health," wrote Bowles, "in pure, dry and stimulating air"; free land, adventure, freedom. The promise compelled people west in waves. No number of busted, disgruntled miners returning east could deter the gold fever when little had been found, and after John H. Gregory's 1859 strike near Central City, the image of Colorado had all the force it would need.

As I rolled into Denver that hot August afternoon, Pikes Peak was plainly visible on the southwest horizon, and I had became a willing, if unknowing, child of the dream.

II. SINKING IN

We have an unknown distance yet to run, an unknown river to explore. What falls there are, we know not; what rocks beset the channel, we know not; what walls rise over the river, we know not. . . . We may conjecture many things.

—John Wesley Powell

The transition from Colorado newcomer to resident is curious. After you arrive, what next?

My answer was to fall in love as quickly as possible. On my first trip, I crossed Kenosha Pass, Trout Creek Pass, Poncha Pass, Slumgullion Pass, and Monarch Pass—plus the Arkansas River and the Rio Grande. Along the Arkansas, north of Poncha Pass, I found a marker commemorating the Christmas 1806 encampment of Pike and his men. "With food perilously low," it read, "on Christmas Eve two hunting parties shot eight buffalo, and Christmas day was spent feasting and repairing equipment." I next drove up Mount Evans—the world's highest auto road (elevation 14,264) with views west to the Continental Divide and east over the foothills and out onto the plains. On my next trip, I vroomed up to Rocky Mountain National Park, drove Trail Ridge Road and breathed in more mountain heights.

On the west slope of the national park, where the road stops snaking switchbacks down Milner Pass and straightens south along the Kawuneechee Valley, I spent my first night under the stars in Colorado. There, in the Timber Creek Campground, I pitched my canvas tent and rolled out a lumpy, Dacron-filled sleeping bag, relic from childhood summers in northern Maine. I was cold; the antique equipment was badly misfit.

During the night, an odd, intermittent din seemed to move around the campground. It sounded like someone blowing loudly on a sometimes piercing, sometimes guttural flute. A campground drunk, I figured and shivered back to sleep. I was wrong.

"Bull elk," a ranger explained next day. "Bugling."

"Bugling?"

"A mating call, a territorial assertion. He has a harem of cows out there. Bugling is his way of letting the other bulls know they're his."

I had wakened at pre-dawn, bone-chilled, and decided the best way to warm myself would be to drive the sports car uphill, hard, with the heater on high. A half dozen curves up in the pale blue light, I came upon two mule deer—a doe, and a fawn relinquishing its spots. With ears back, they bounced off on all fours into an aspen-choked gulch. Above timberline, another mule deer, a huge buck, crossed Trail Ridge Road ahead of me and stopped on a tundra knoll silhouetted against the sky.

"Mossback in velvet," a dapper man who pulled up behind me called him.

"Mossback?"

"A big, old buck. They grow new antlers every year. They have a soft cover until they're full size. That's velvet."

Drive on, the voice said, and so I did. Berthoud Pass, Loveland Pass, Independence Pass, Tennessee Pass. La Veta Pass, with the wind blowing around me and the sun streaming down. On a Conoco road map with magic markers I began redlining all the roads I had driven. Within a year it looked like a spider web in shambles. I kept track of the places I crossed the Continental Divide and got the count quickly up beyond a dozen. And drove on.

New perceptions for an Easterner arrived West: First, distances were less. Growing up, a seventy-five-mile trip was some undertaking; in Colorado you did it in an hour when roads were straight, two when they were not. Second, vision was longer. Seeing sixty miles in a direction at a glance, facing that much space, was at first a shock but progressively reassuring because of all that fit together at once. Third, possibilities were greater. Topping a mountain pass—having the panorama on the far side rise and spread out before me—was like revelation. Each time, another new world. I could not get enough.

I finally traded the sports car in on a ragtop jeep and kept driving—now learning to lurch along rocky, rutted, gutted, gullied, muddy former mountain mine roads. Still manic in love, full of heady romance, the champagne travelogue phase of the Colorado experience.

Gradually, the state began to take on a shape, gain a configuration. I had come to be in the mountains; now individual ranges sorted out from the generic mass of the Rockies, distinguished themselves from one another. The Gore Range above Silverthorne and Vail: a single, fine, serrated line of peaks. The Sawatch behind Buena Vista: massive, blocky heights with long approach ridges and Mount Elbert, at 14,431, Colorado's tallest. The Mosquito Range up back of Fairplay with its rolling bare summits and names drawn from Civil War politics. The Sangre de Cristo Range, "the Blood of Christ Mountains," named by early Spanish for the crimson sunrises so common above them— boney, fault-block peaks bristling with angles, points, and sharp edges. And my favorite: the San Juan Range, a volcanic maze, spineless, undisciplined, covering an area greater than two Connecticuts. The sheer extent of this range is part of its appeal; in no other part of Colorado can you hike peak or ridge and be so utterly surrounded by mountains, ridges, cirques, aretes, rims, and tarns. But their visual geometry was what excited most. The San Juan's mountains are named after their form. Here is a quick, exemplary inventory: Twin Thumbs, Turret, Tower, Chimney, Courthouse, Whitehouse, Dome. Needle, Arrow, Knife Point. Lizard Head, Coxcomb, Wildhorse, Wolf Tooth. Heisshorn, Wetterhorn, Matterhorn. The Hand. Teakettle, Pool Table. Lone Cone.

The state, I learned, has more than forty ranges in all: some famous, others obscure. On maps, I scanned many recesses, nooks, and remote spurs, and where my jeep would go, I sought them out.

My discoveries partially atoned for the jarring jeep trips. I had come upon bugling elk, and deer in velvet in Rocky Mountain National Park; I walked among wildflowers in a profusion that exceeded any I imagined to exist. Some were close, wild cousins to species I had seen in rows in weeded gardens as I grew up back East; columbine and lupine struck me first. It had not occurred to me that they could grow quite well on their own without the aid of sprinkler, fertilizer, or trowel. The variety of wildflowers and the way they mingled together added to my surprise. They seemed like a fabric of color spread over the mountainside, a bright batik; ten or a dozen different species were in bloom, blanketing the color spectrum; when a breeze moved down a slope, the entire slanting meadow rippled and whipped—producing the same image of wind you get watching it move over the surface of a lake.

On a trip to Cloyses Lake, I also got a close-up feel for a mountain range: the Sawatch, with the huge symmetrical bulk of its landforms that so distinguish it. It is one thing to gaze on mountains pictorially from without, and quite another to wander around in their gut. Less than a mile southwest of the lake is a reach of the Continental Divide: a long, gray ridge dropping sharply toward the lake. Its profile is that of a large, pushed down hump—not a dramatic sight, merely solid and strong. East and west are Missouri

Mountain and Mount Huron—large, mounded, 14,000-foot peaks with great, rounded shoulders sweeping upward out of sight. To the north, across Clear Creek's canyon, is Mount Hope and beside it Quail Mountain, another pair of weighty, clean-lined mountains. In none of this was there much fineness of detail or delicacy of form; instead, I left Cloyses Lake with images of great size and mass.

Though I did not sense it then, a transition was beginning. Early on, I had accumulated impressions and gathered facts, moving steadily from one place to the next, drawn on by the state's diversity and extent. Colorado was land to be cased, sized up, checked out. At Cloyses Lake, I felt a different pull, which at first seemed only an impediment to my headlong rush around the state. My stereotyped view had held that Colorado equals mountains; flatland diversity was not worth checking out. I was wrong.

Between the Park and Rawah ranges along the Wyoming line and extending south toward mid-state is a chain of three broad mountain parks—North Park, South Park, Middle Park. Too broad to be called valleys, they appear misplaced expanses of prairie, raised high in the mountains, given more rainfall, and ringed with peaks. The parks are large, as much as sixty miles between opposite foothills.

South Park, marked on very early maps as Bayou Salado because of its salt deposits, is the highest and largest of the three, with base elevation at 10,000 feet, and area nearly 130 square miles. Long ago plains animals moved up to the three parks: buffalo once upon a time, pronghorn antelope still, and in North and Middle parks, sage grouse. South Park is more grassy; Middle and North parks tend toward sage.

The floor of North Park is level only in contrast to its surrounding rim of peaks and a long, forested, northwest-southeast ridge bisecting its upper reach. The terrain seems in constant motion: a land of dips, sweeps, and swells. Nothing is prominent enough to be called a knoll or gulch, just gradual rises and wide draws. The cover is largely sage, with shortgrass in old, saucer-shaped buffalo wallows.

Then I discovered hunting. One morning I had the cross-hairs of my scope on a fine buck with tall horns, but while I breathed and steadied for a shot, he receded into a veil of snow. When I last saw him, his dark horns and nose had reduced to faint marks in a field of white. The rest of him was invisible. I never saw him move; he just faded. I did not see him again. But I learned that hunting is more than just the kill; it is the discipline, the concentration, the discoveries.

During those years, like the increasingly more ample and accurate state maps of the 1860s and 1870s, my sense of Colorado was sharpening while the image and glitter began to wear off. Newcomers have the capacity to see this state as exotic; natives do not. I bought a backpack, and the pace of my travels slowed. Mimicking Pike and his kind,

I made a casual point of seeking places where I could imagine I was the first human ever to set foot. This meant spending time nosing in wilderness—bushwhacking, rock-whacking, getting off any semblance of a beaten path. At the same time, I returned to sites visited four and five years earlier—and discovered texture and density I had previously rushed past. I swapped the ragtop jeep for a hardtop, then a subcompact sedan. I explored afoot, on touring skis, rafts, in a canoe.

I rafted a wild river, the Dolores. As I was drawn from the mountains by hunting, so I was lured to Colorado's redrock, slickrock country by water—rapid, flatwater, eddy, and chute. As North, Middle and South parks were prairie high among mountains, so the Dolores country was Utah desert butted against their western flank. Santa Fe traders noted and named this 250-mile river in the mid-1700s: *El Río de Nuestra Señora de los Dolores*, "The River of Our Lady of Sorrows," a place most generous in its gifts, and exacting in its demands.

Our ninety-mile journey sank us first into a deep foothill canyon; then through an intricate, plunging rapid named Snaggletooth; past increasingly vivid outcrops of red and tawny sandstone; beneath ponderosa pine, box elder, pinon pine, juniper, tamarisk, willow, scrub oak. On we swept with one world, briefly known, receding behind us, and another, unknown, looming ahead. More rafts flipped; a third wrapped helplessly around a bridge pier near the one-restaurant, two-gas pump settlement of Slick Rock. All in the party were scared. Some lament the passing of Colorado's last free-roaming grizzly because with him went a fear that makes wilderness numinous and alien. In untested rapids and overturned, racked-up rafts, a kindred fear is quite far from extinct. All twelve of us were on the Dolores for the first time, explorers sometimes wishing we were not. A night's sleep and half a day's drift below the bridge pier we passed into another realm. This was Slick Rock Canyon, thirty-three miles long, the third of five on the Dolores. Here the river is smooth and tan, silt loaded. The rock comes in massive chunks, folds, and walls, all classic southwest in color: brick red, chocolate brown, yellow, pink, buff, ochre, maroon. Moving water, still rock.

There are places—notches, draws, tributary washes, and side canyons—where you can climb the 1,800 feet from river to rim and see the snow-crested peaks of the San Juan Range to the east. Down in the canyon, mountains are unthinkable; an immense distance away. The play of reflected color on water produced a steady liquid mosaic. We saw mergansers, phalaropes, and Canada geese that lumbered, honking, into flight. Rockforms shifted constantly: down at the water's edge, on the median walls and slopes, atop the rims.

The June afternoon was warm, the sun near solstice and direct. Very easy to become dreamy, woozy, and sink into a profound, relaxed state of disorientation—losing all sense of direction, distance, and time. Occasionally, we passed something ashore that pulled us back to consciousness: a lizard on a rock, a juniper twisted like flame, a thunderbird pictograph in a cave.

Wilderness is what I value most in Colorado. In my early years here, I knew nothing of wilderness either as fact or concept. Gradually, however, a common thread emerged from seemingly disparate experiences, and the clearer it became, the more I was hooked, compelled, eager to push on. The journey now seems a sequence of perceptions, each adding dimension, none detracting from the other.

Wilderness as travelogue. This is the tourist perception, the distant view of scenery and the picturesque—uplifting, bracing, gorgeous, beautiful, sublime.

Wilderness as opportunity. As a child of America, my passage from the East to Colorado to wilderness has been toward an elemental opportunity to explore. New worlds to learn: new names, new processes, new relationships.

Wilderness as contrast. This perception sees wilderness as escape, a psychological haven. An alternative to partitions and walls which insulate and close in. A respite from the driving staccato of telephones, buzzers, clocks, signs, sirens, and horns. An occasion to relax, slow down, dawdle, do nothing, be.

Wilderness as moral ground. Wilderness is neutral, but areas of wide-open possibility require that one decide and act. There is virtue in an environment—mountain valley, rock face, mossy draw, or sneaky, dry canyon—that pushes one to sift alternatives and make choices with consequences both immediate and real.

Wilderness as roots. Wilderness is not just an alluring emptiness—a black hole drawing us ever in. It has tangible reality that can be kicked, smelled, and swum in. It is a place of vision, song, aroma, taste, and touch—of texture and chemistry, instinct and feel. It is a place of hunger as known by hummingbird and hawk, or fear as known by meadow mouse, of time as known by migrating butterflies. It is a set of rhythms, processes, and relations—finely meshed, always evolving, hinting at our ends, giving us a sense of belonging, the only home we will ever have here and now.

III. CLOSING UP

What's the use kickin? I got none coming. When I came West I got the cream. Let the come latelys have the skimmilk.

—Charles M. Russell (1926)

In midsummer 1952, in a high hole in the San Juan Range known as Starvation Gulch, Colorado's last wild grizzly bear was killed. He was a young boar, two years old, weighing maybe 250 pounds—not a very awesome specimen of *Ursus horribilis*, but then terminal cases rarely are. His crime was mauling and dining on a number of domestic sheep grazing in his territory.

The event marks a passage in Colorado history, a tangible shift from the wild toward the developed. "Grizzly," it said, "your claim to this state is hereby terminated. Your particular brand of wildness is no longer tolerable. You are too alien, too predatory; you range too freely and far. Sorry. We no longer have enough space."

Colorado has been and is closing up. The state faces a transformation as basic as when white men first settled its soil. As it becomes increasingly developed, it loses not only its wild valleys and rich basins, but also its homey cowtowns and a steady, rhythmic pace tied to the land. The loss is of openness, not only of space, but of personality, human character.

Causes of the process are two. Nearly a century and a half ago, gold and silver boomed the Pikes Peak country in the national eye; today, coal, oil shale, uranium, and natural gas boost it as a national energy epicenter—a fact that brings not only direct environmental havoc, but also more jobs, more people, less space. Meanwhile, the feeling that both the East Coast and the West are too hectic, crowded, and cluttered— basically unlivable—makes Colorado and its ambience still appear, to many, a promised land. Colorado has become a vortex of national desires where versions of the good life chafe, and in any case, move toward a point where dream (now the illusion of plenty) exceeds the capacity of the land and its life to fulfill it.

At best, only about 15 percent of the state is still wild, part of which is now protected under the National Parks System and the Forest Service.

Colorado is still rich in moderate areas of wild, open space—suspended in its history between a past we found and a future we desire. There is much more wilderness here than in my native New England, where it exists only in cramped lots, reservations, and preserves. But there is much less than in Alaska, where wilderness has been set aside in intact ecosystems and grand sweeps of openness large enough to honor the grizzly. Colorado is midpoint between these two poles.

In the end, this state's final decision on its wilderness will, like Pike's encounter with his peak, be as symbolic as it is real. It will be a decision not just about land preservation, but about the basic design of our entire civilization, our way of life: the balance point it has chosen between the wild and the developed. As such, Colorado will become the nation's exemplary mix of the open and the regulated, of contrast and sameness, of choice and coercion. And, ultimately, Colorado will serve as evidence of the degree to which we, as an American people, choose to honor our deepest roots.

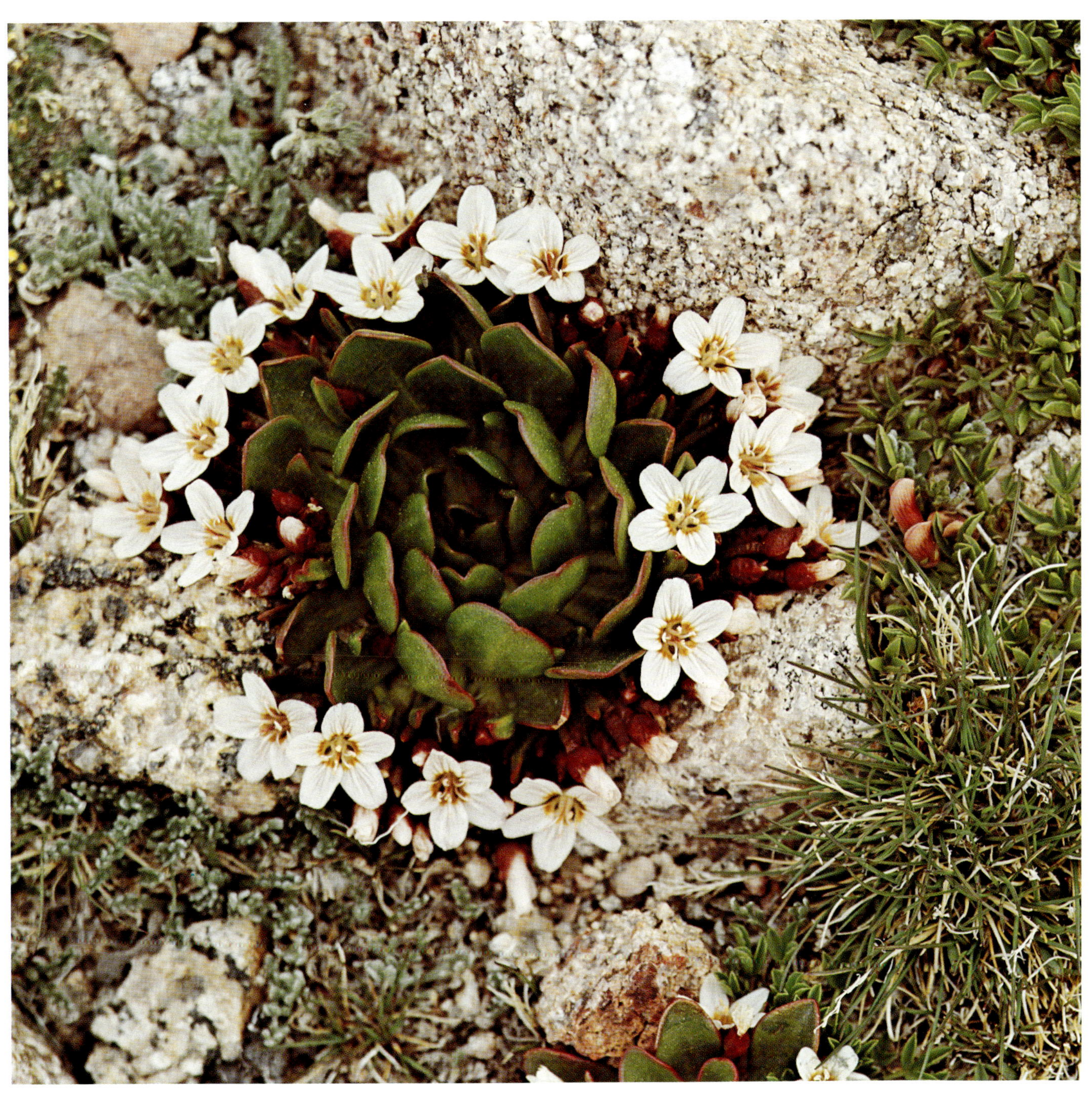

▲ Tundra supports a dense growth of conspicuously flowering dwarf plants.
▶ ▶ Below the Crestone Peaks, dunes in the San Luis Valley reach more than seven hundred feet high.

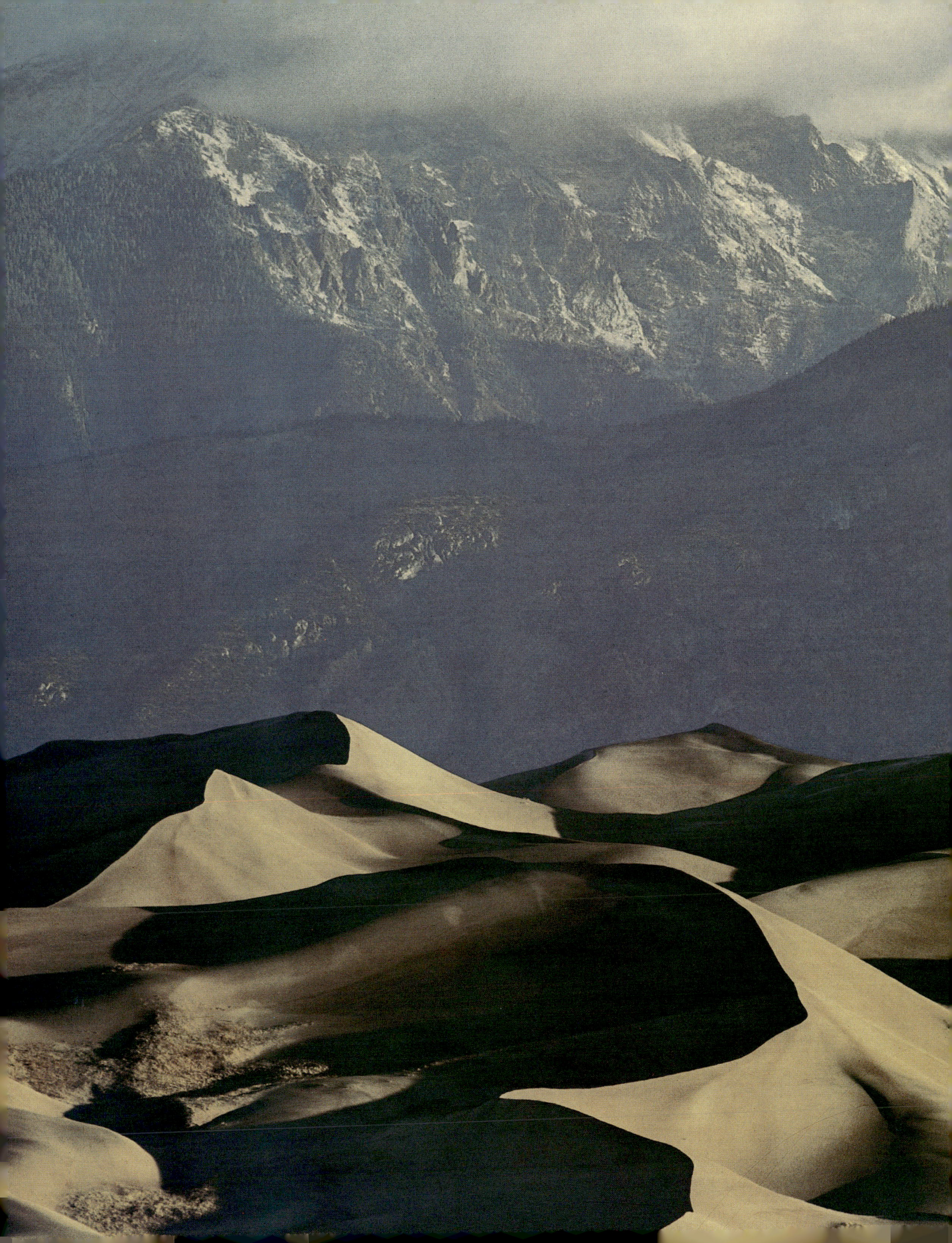

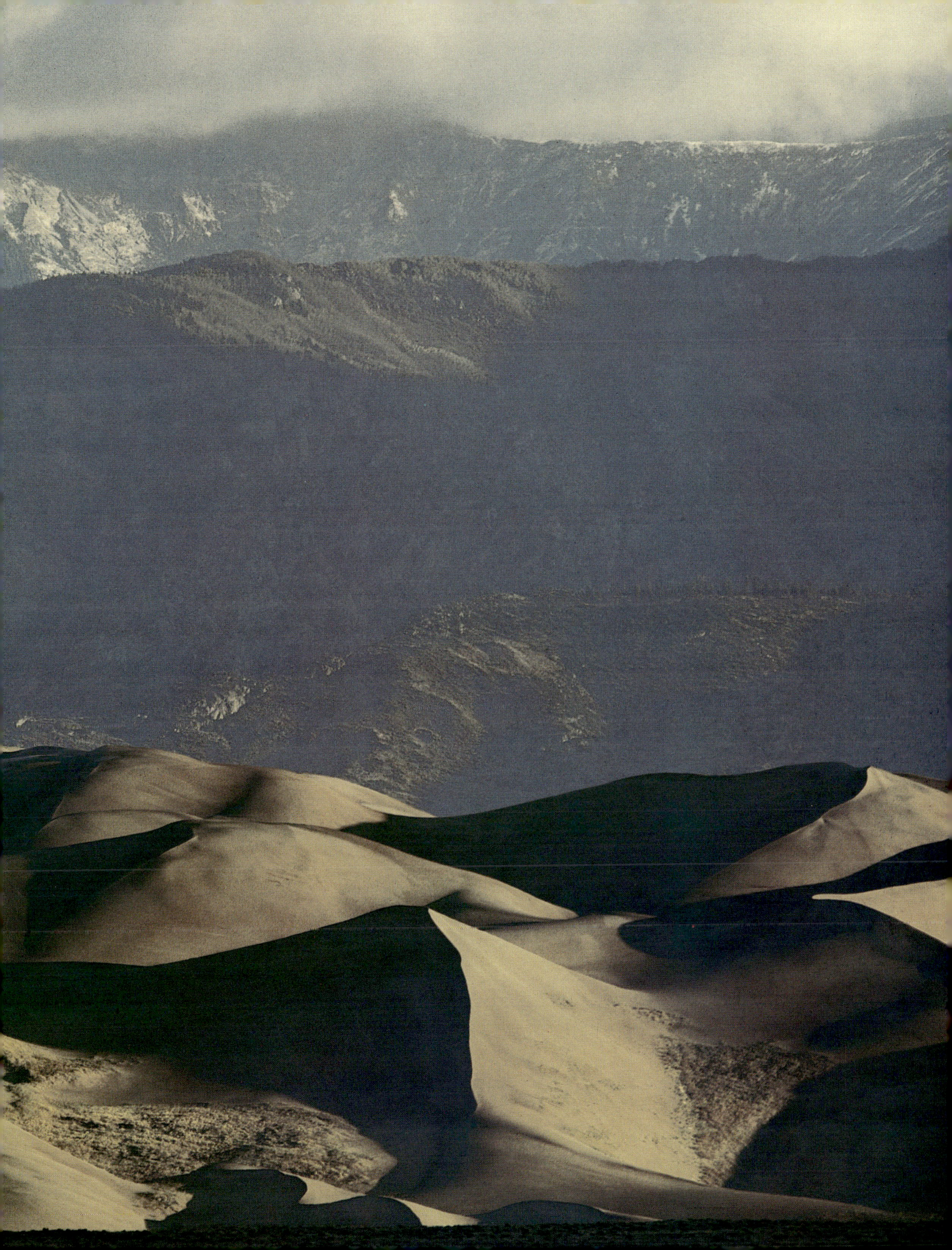

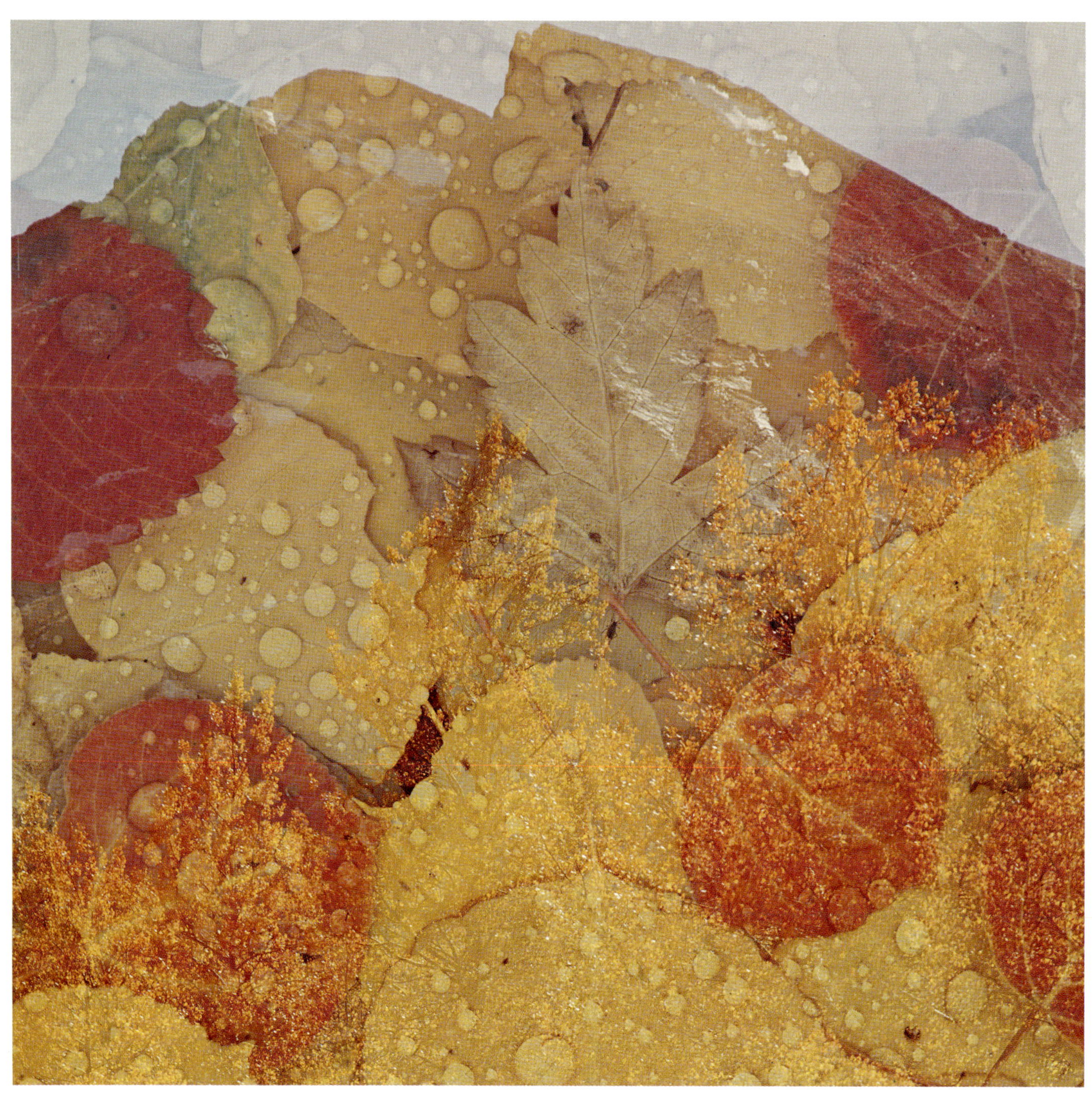

▲ High in the Sawatch Range, the twilight of autumn colors soon transcends another season.

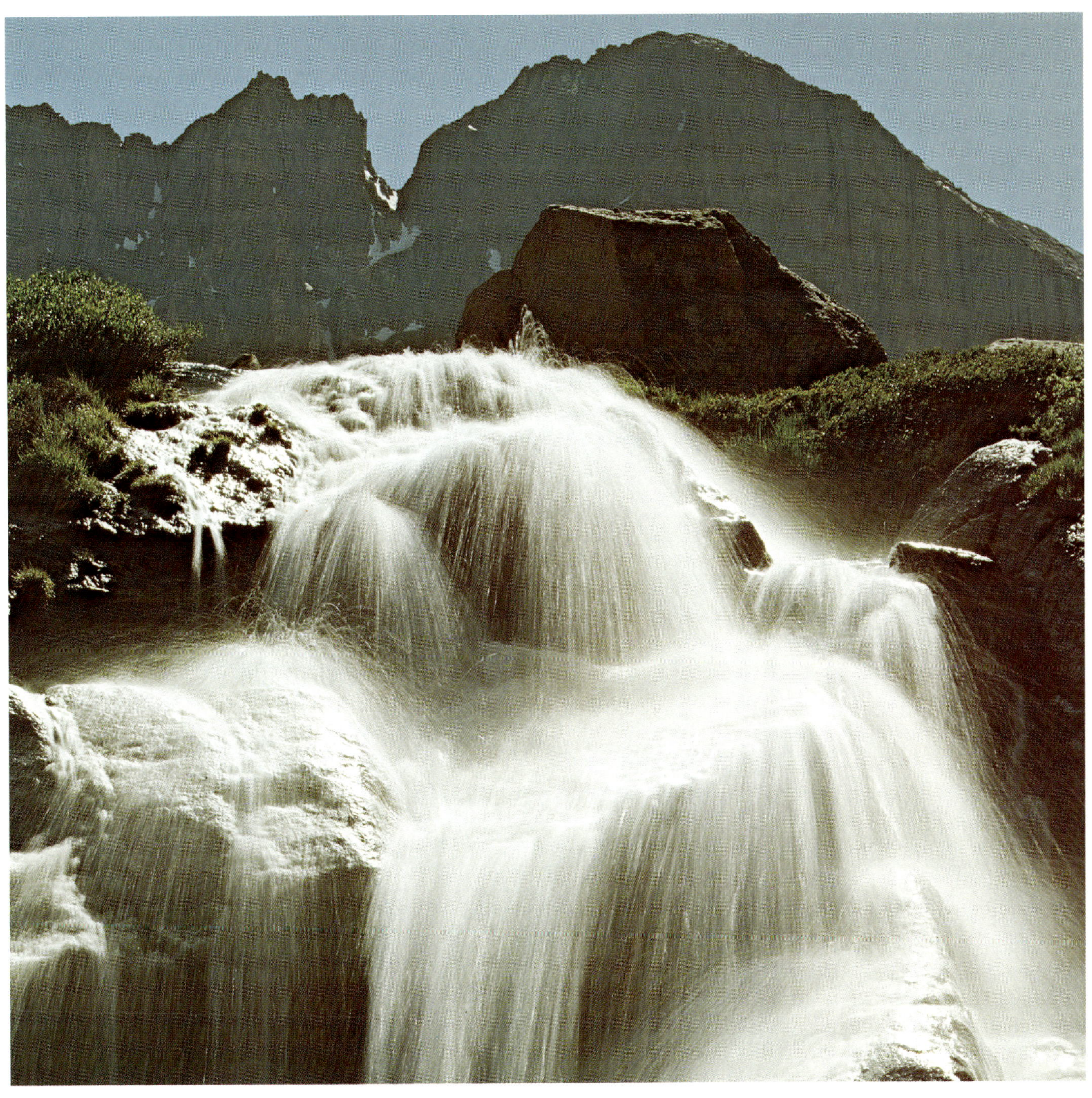

▲ Below the northeast face of 14,256-foot Longs Peak, Roaring Fork tumbles over rocks at Chasm Lake.
► ► Spring summons the leafing out of the plains cottonwood along lower elevations of the Sneffels Range.

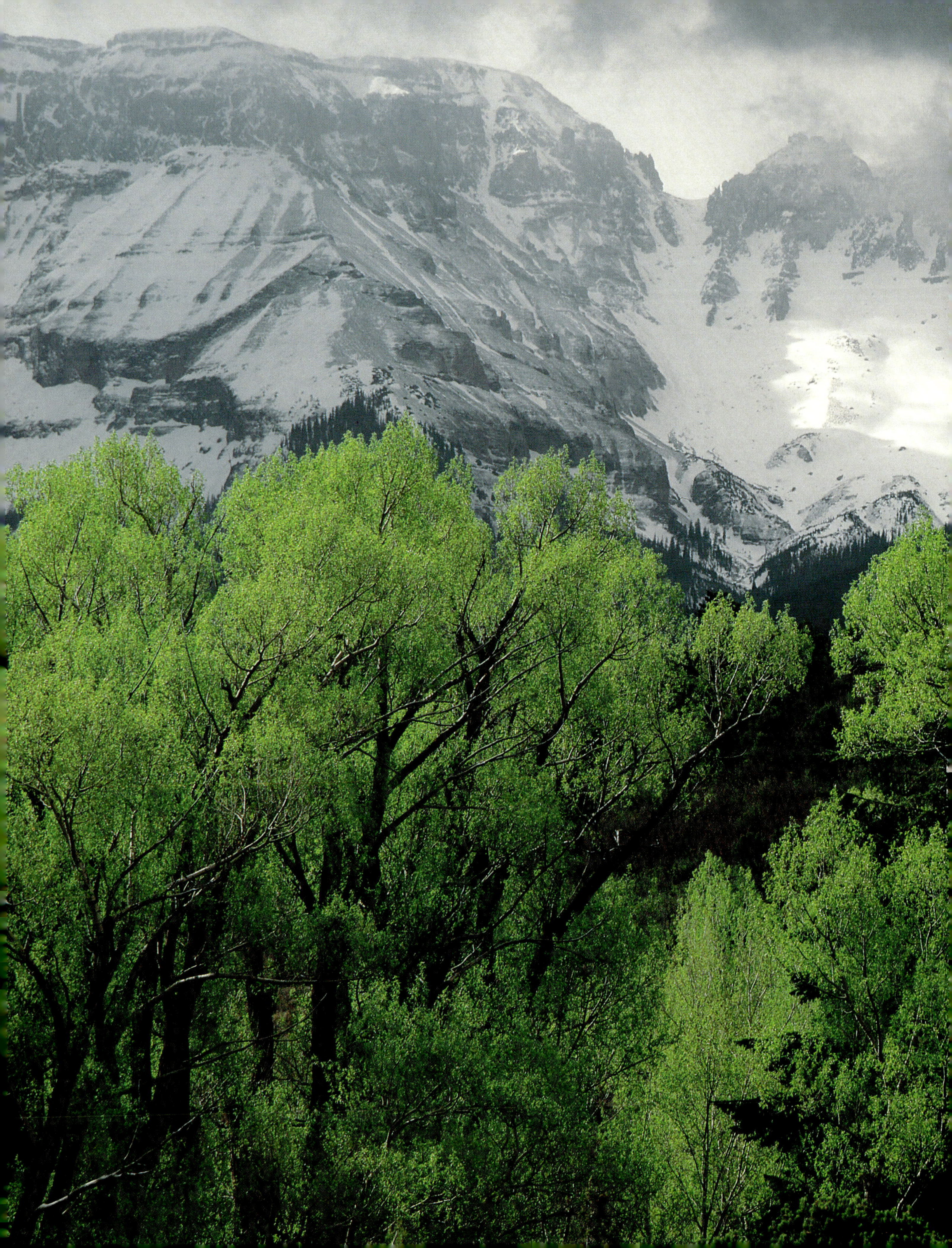

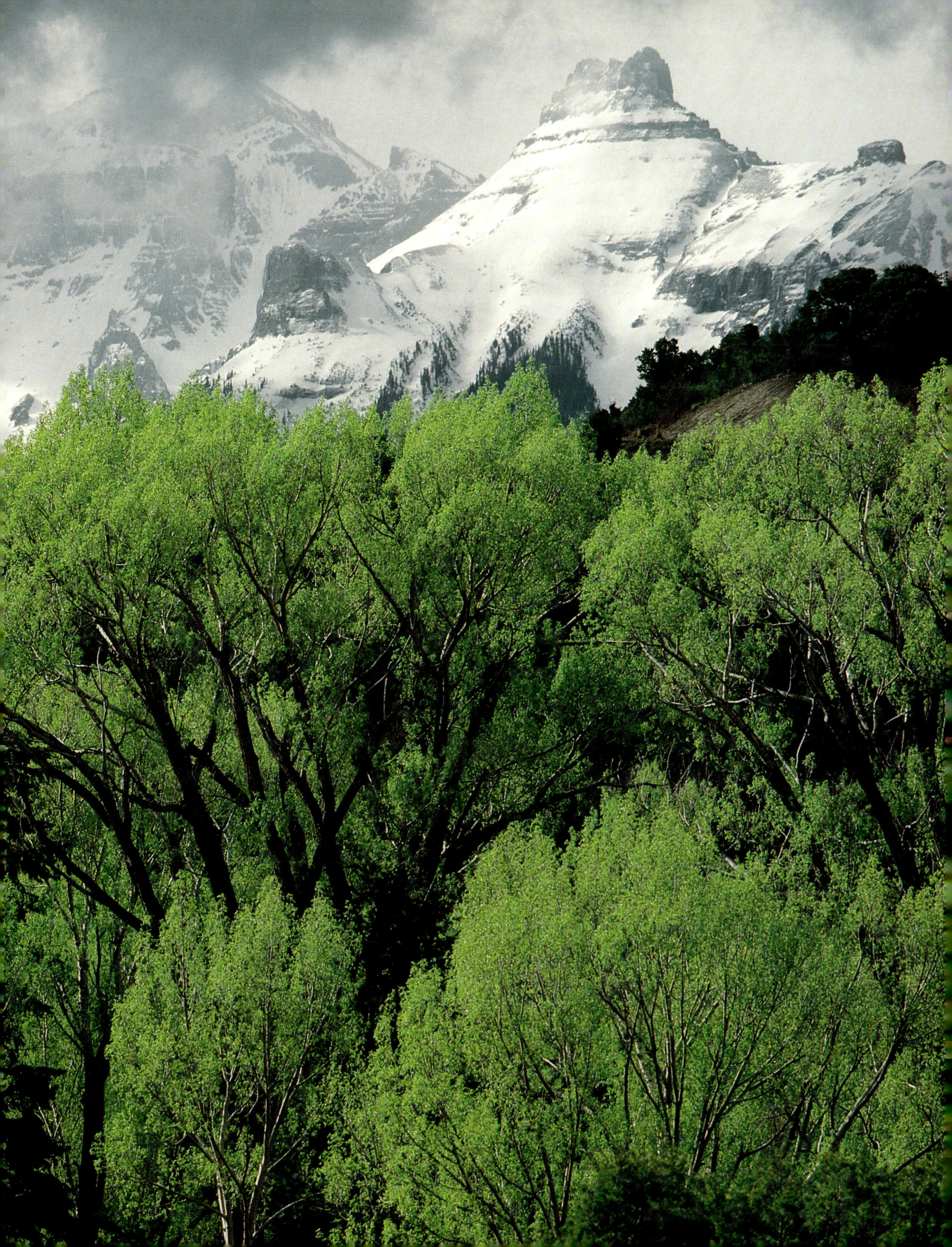

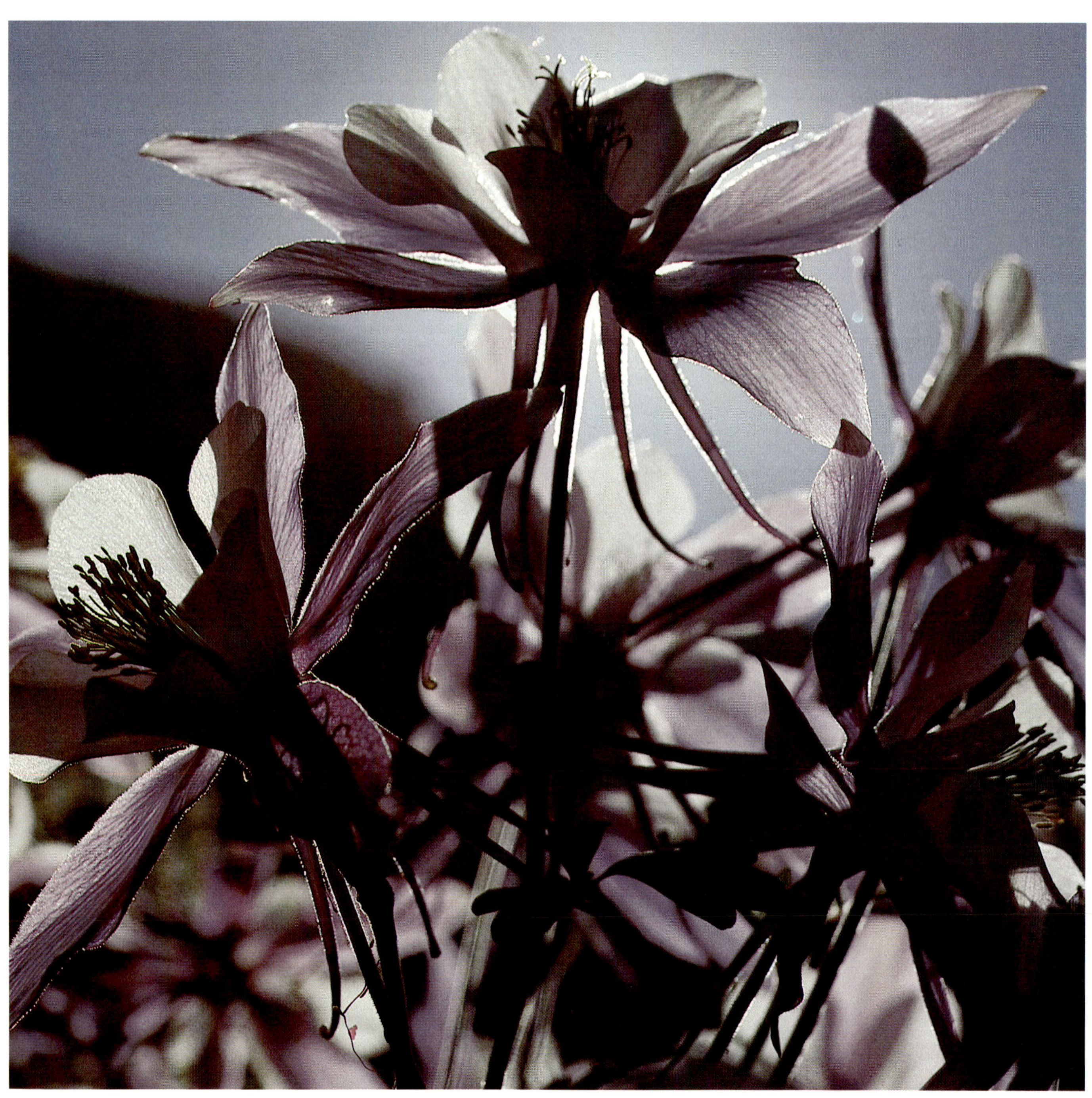

▲ Against a brilliant sun, blue columbine gives translucent relief.

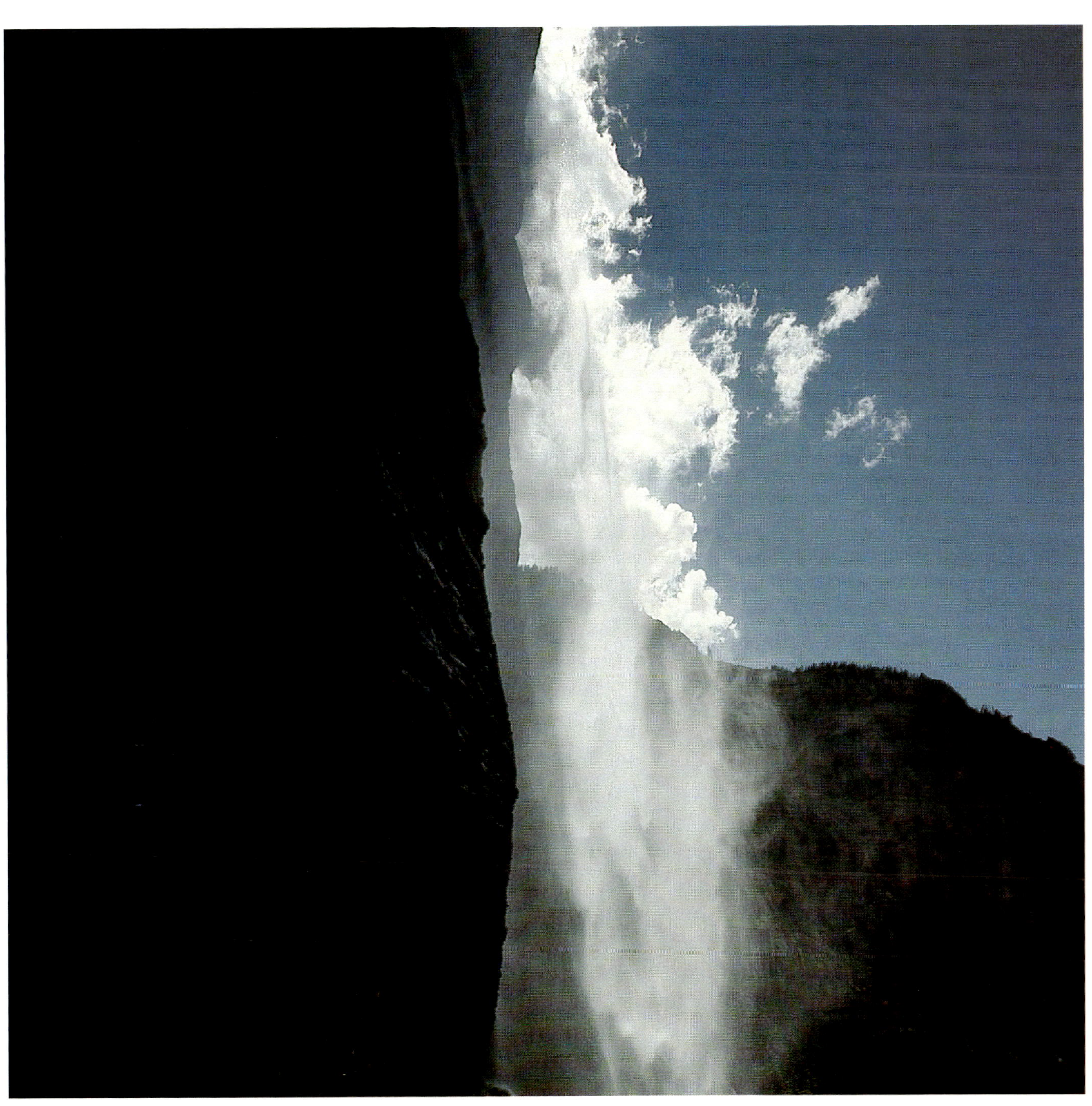

▲ Above Telluride, Bridal Veil Falls lets its "veil" down over the cliffs to the valley floor.

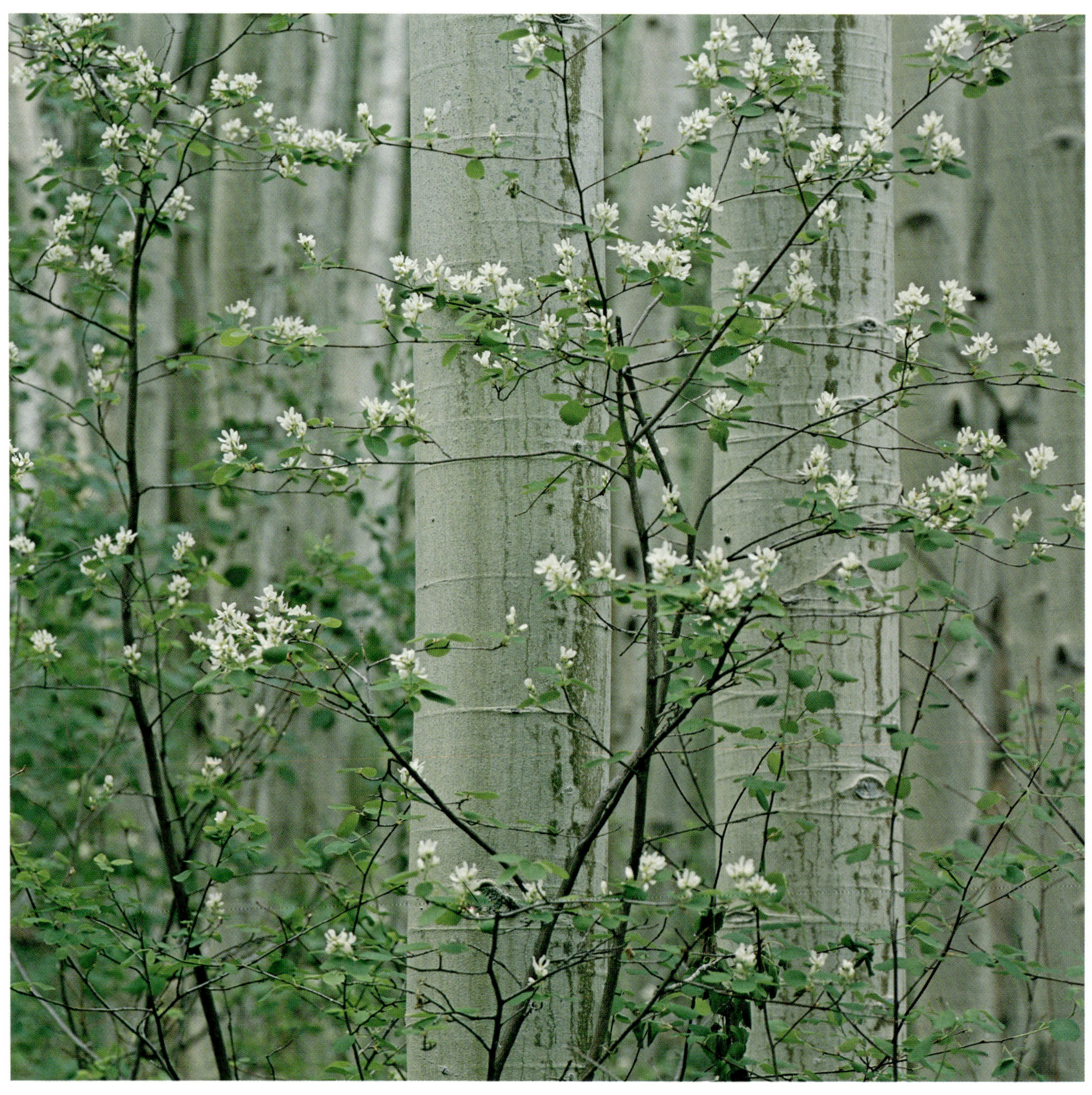

▲ Early blooming serviceberry graces an aspen forest in late May.
▶ Quaking aspen glows in September's waning light.

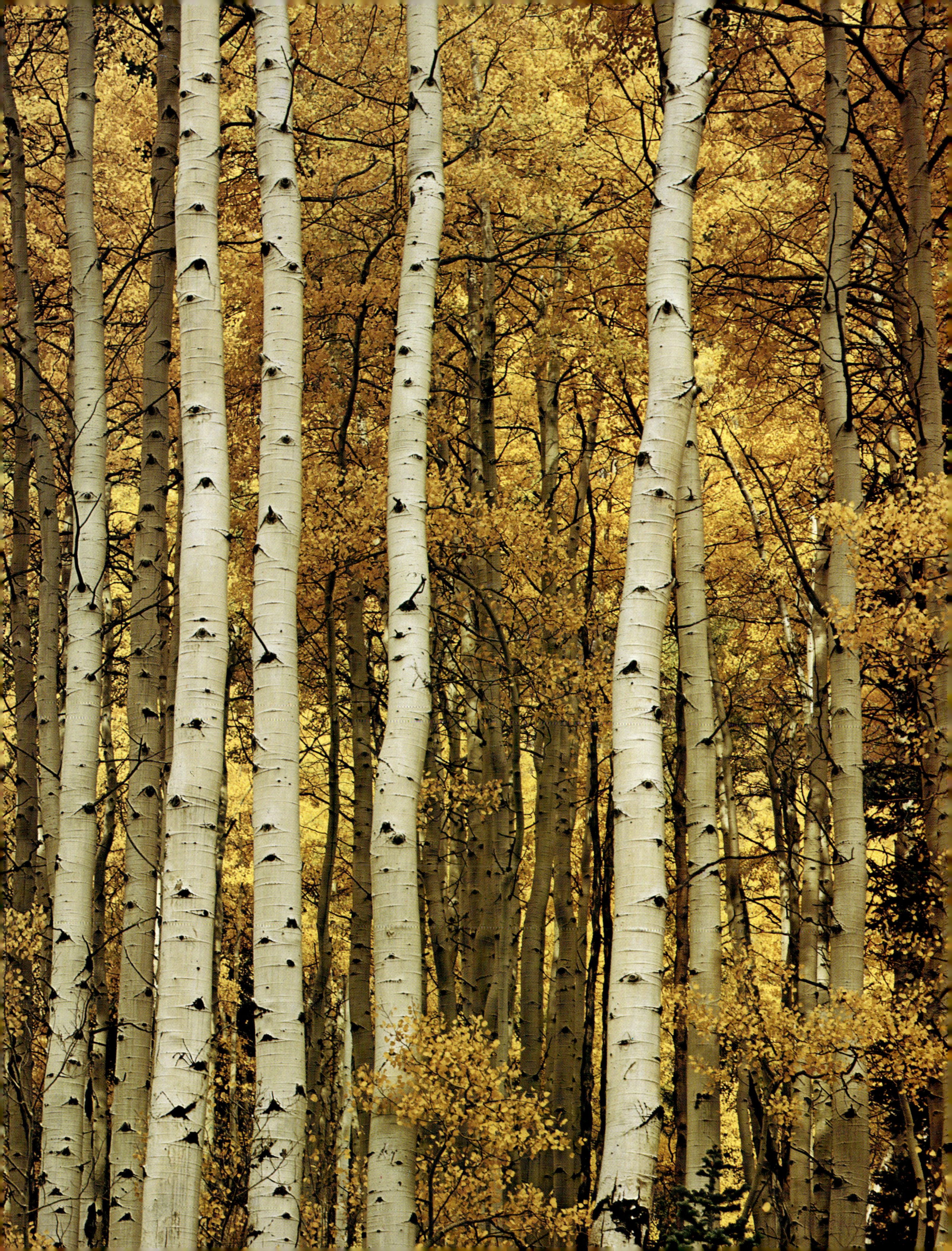

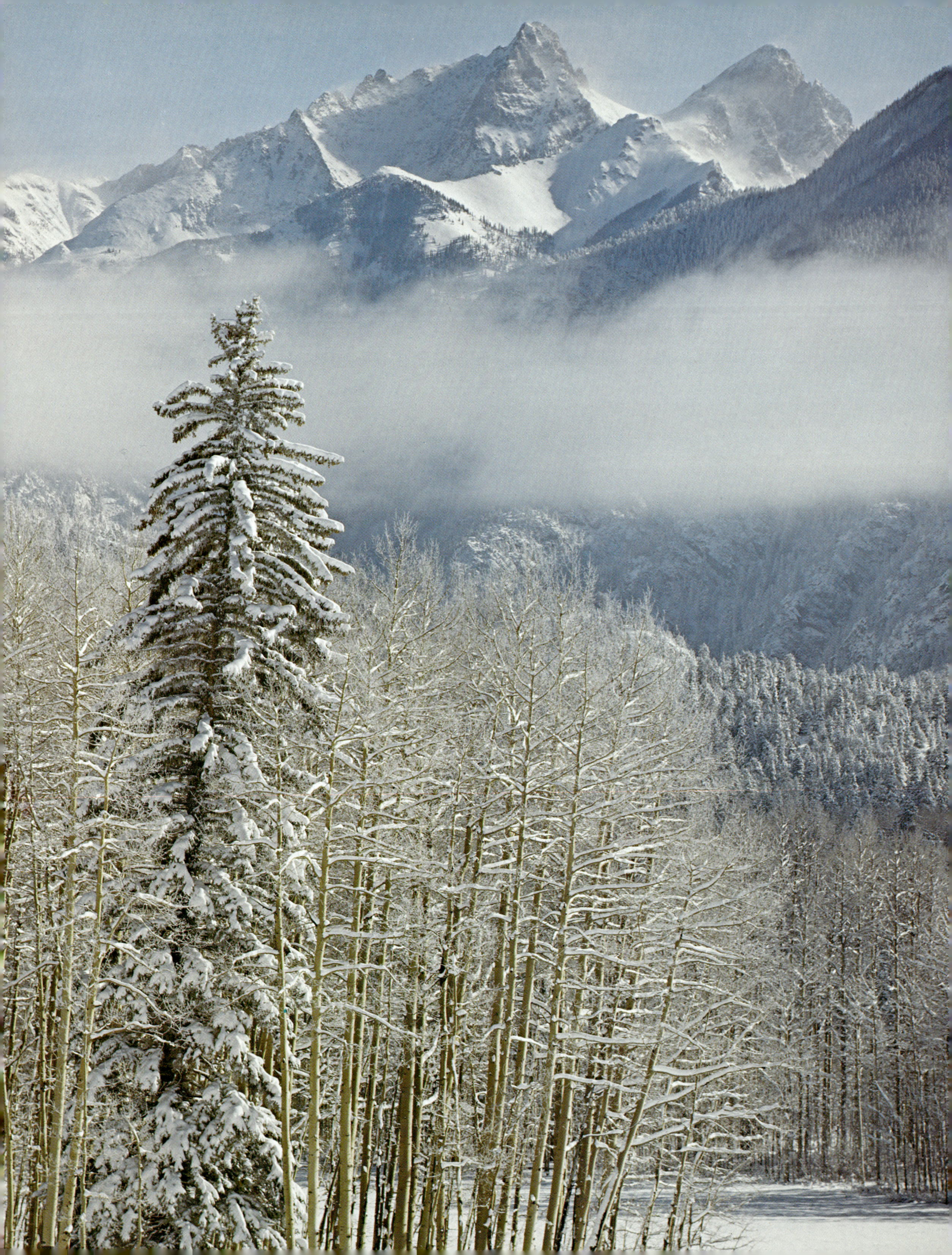

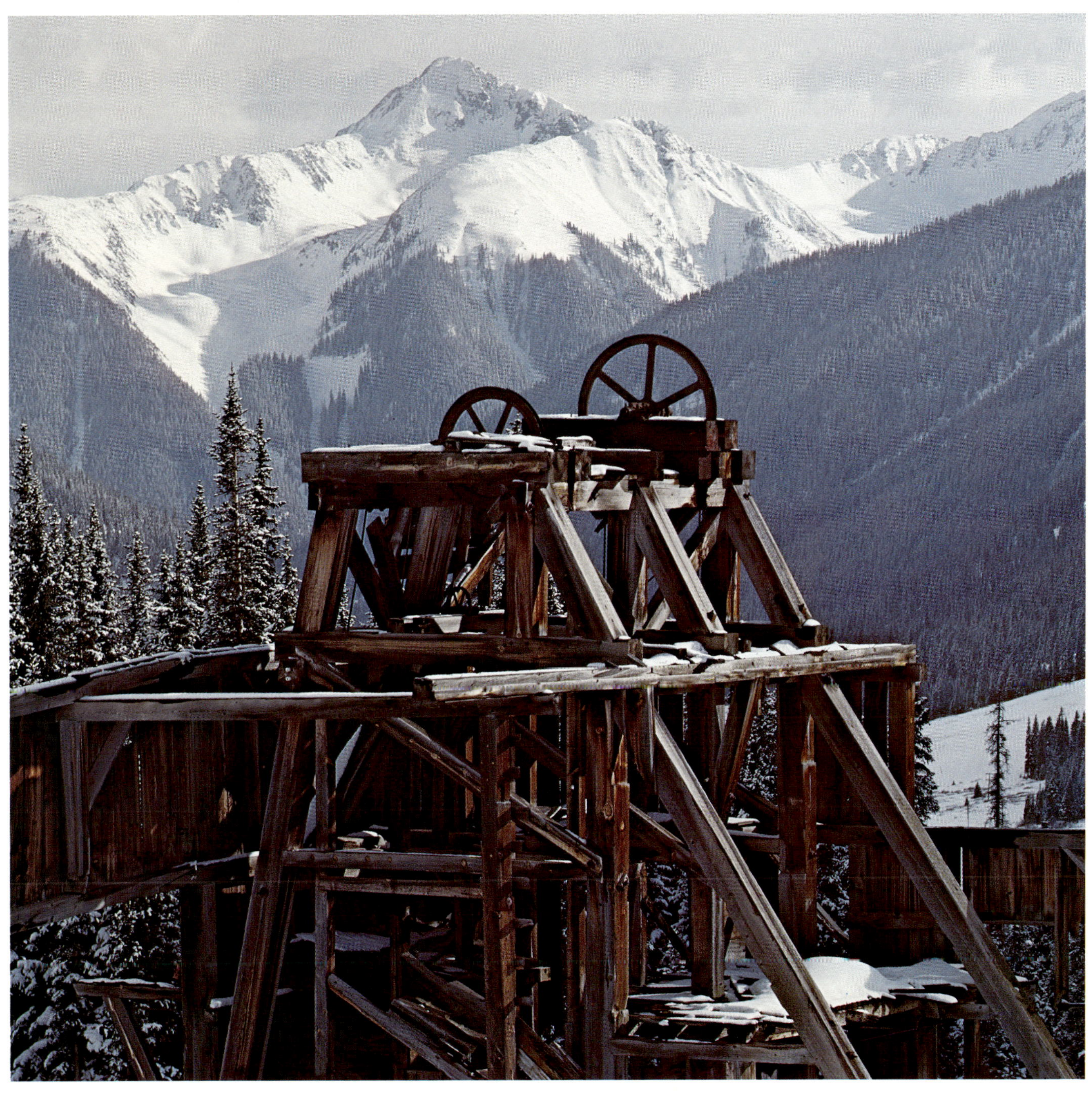

◄ In Weminuche Wilderness Area, Pigeon and Turret peaks of the Needle Mountains reach nearly 14,000 feet.
▲ Skeleton headworks and 12,585-foot Bear Mountain tower above Mineral Creek canyon, in Red Mountain Pass.

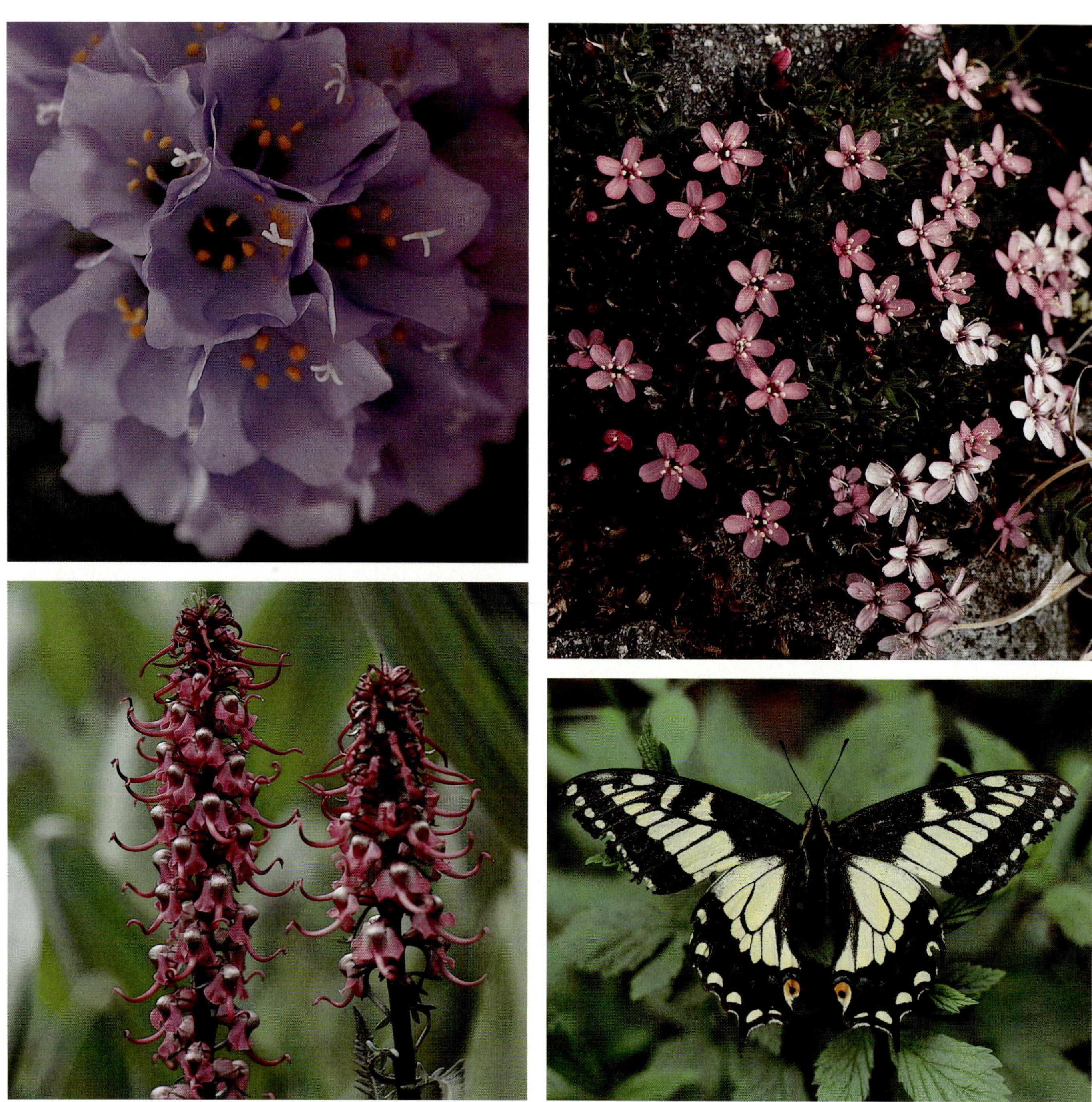

▲ Wildflowers and butterflies dot timberline country: sky pilot, moss campion, elephanthead, swallowtail butterfly.
► In the San Juan Mountains, a quiet pool reflects 13,738-foot Grizzly Peak and 12,968-foot Engineer Mountain.

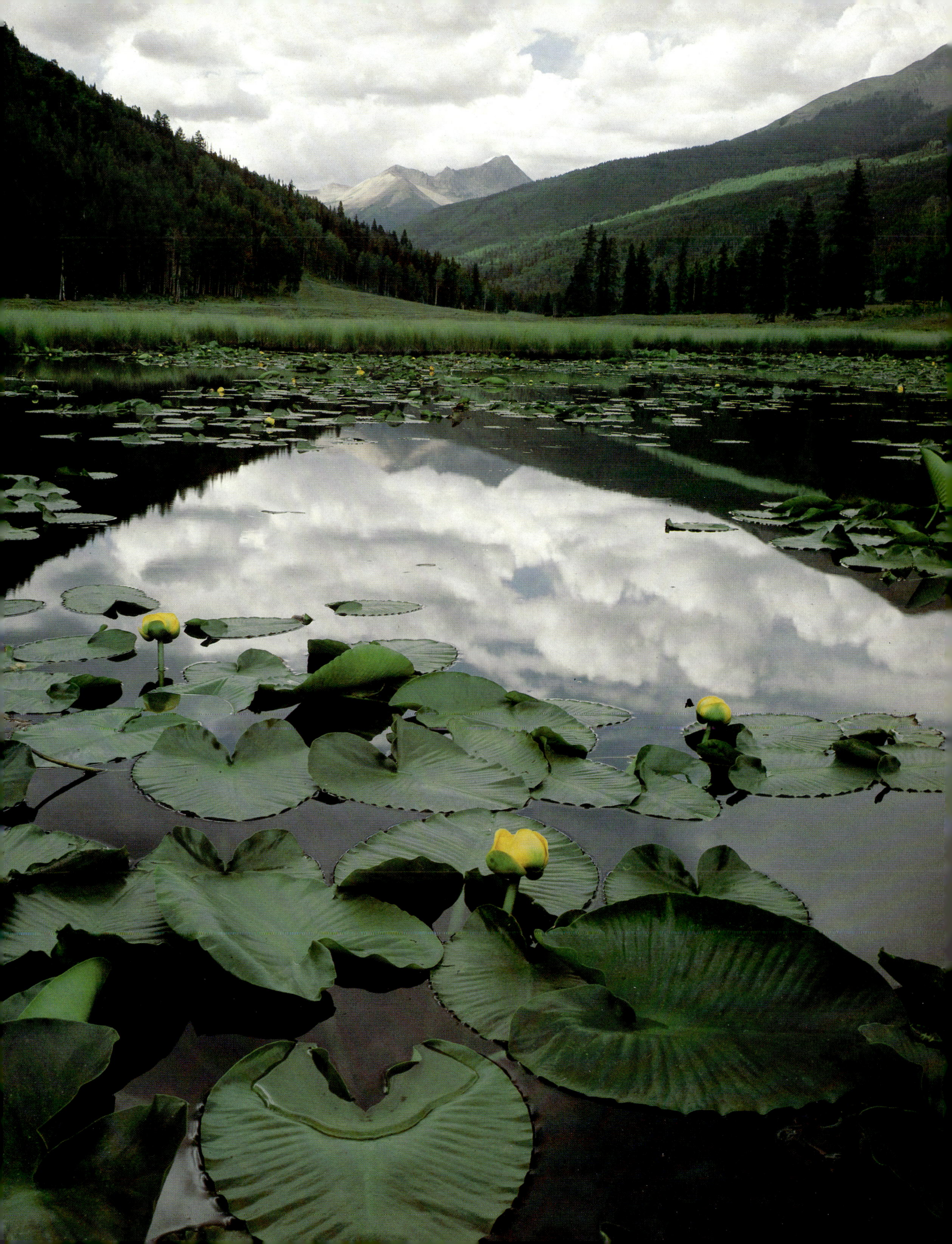

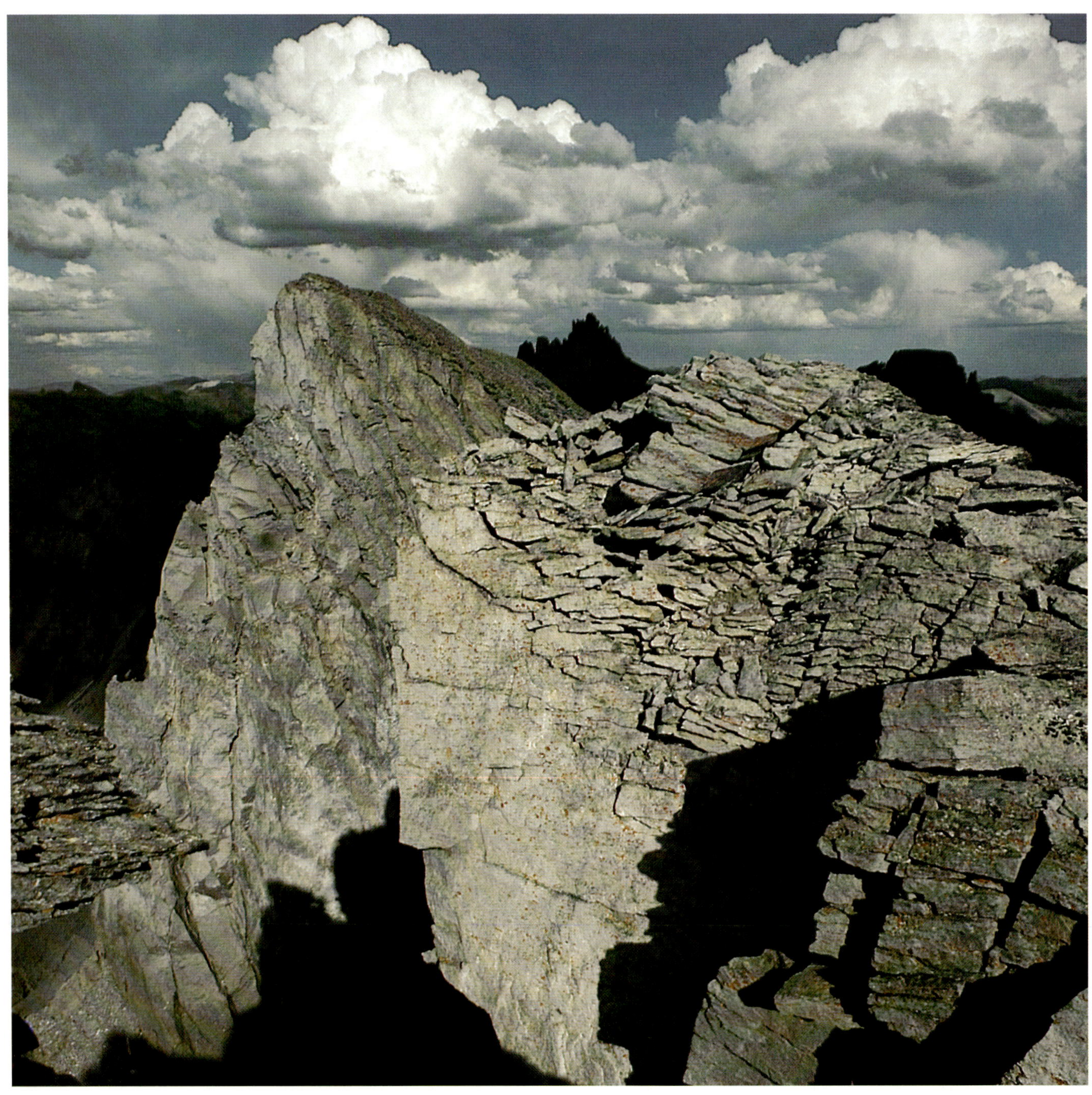

▲ Teakettle Mountain and Potosi Peak are visible from Cirque Peak's slowly crumbling summit.

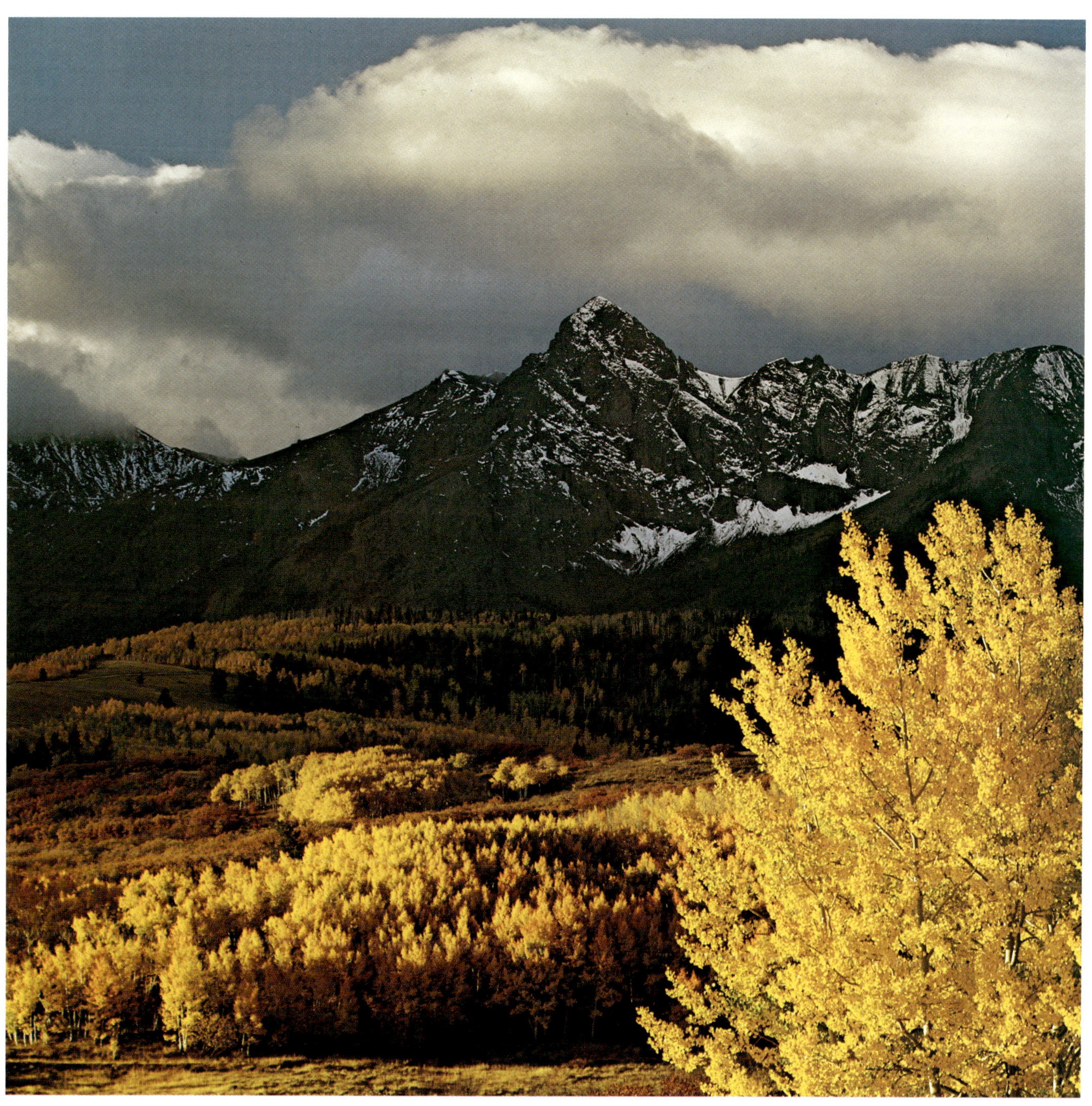

▲ Aspen stands are emblazoned against flanks of the Sneffels Range in Dallas Divide.

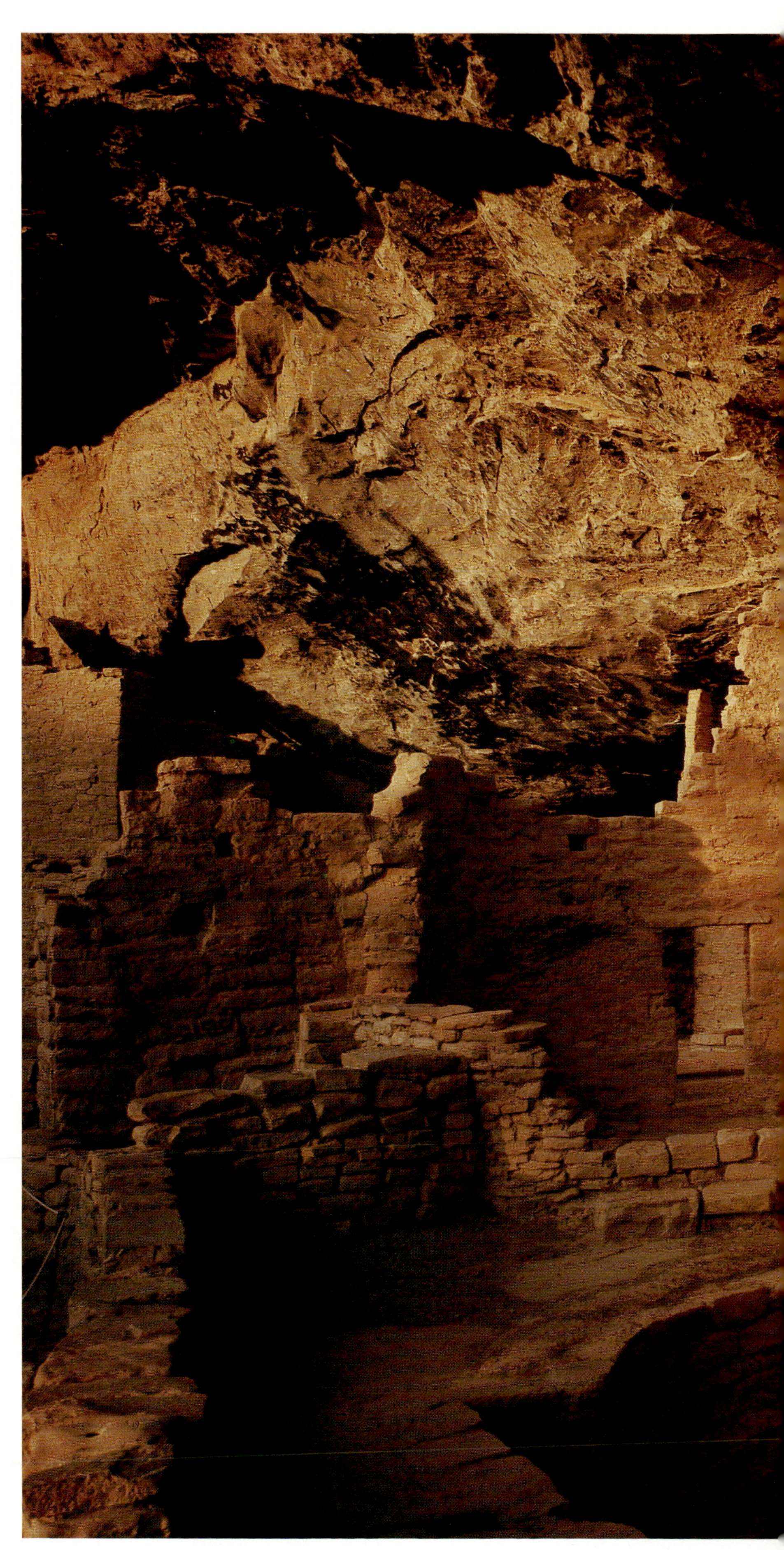

THE
RED ROCK

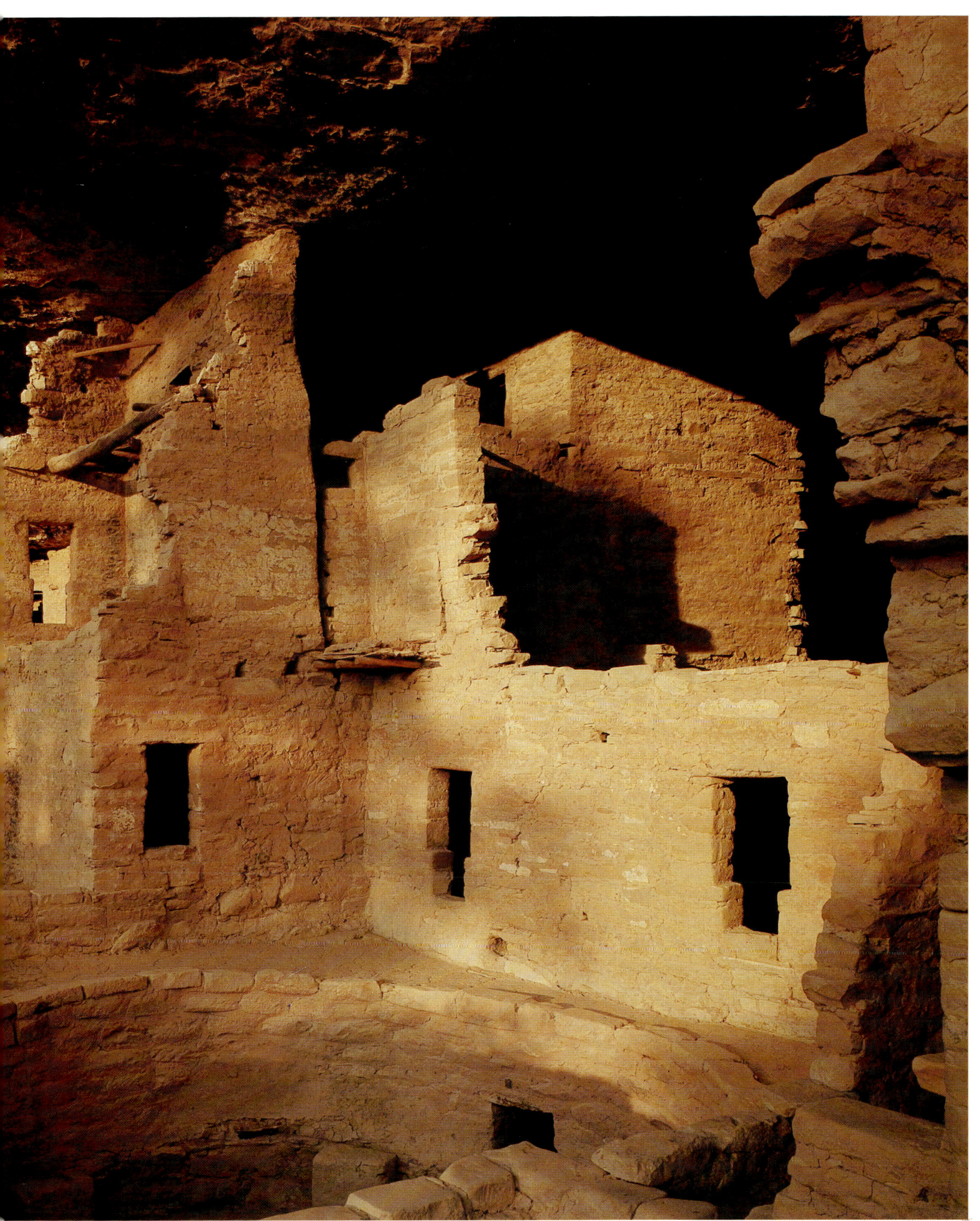

▲ Spruce Tree House, built by the Anasazi, is situated under a sandstone lip in Mesa Verde National Park.

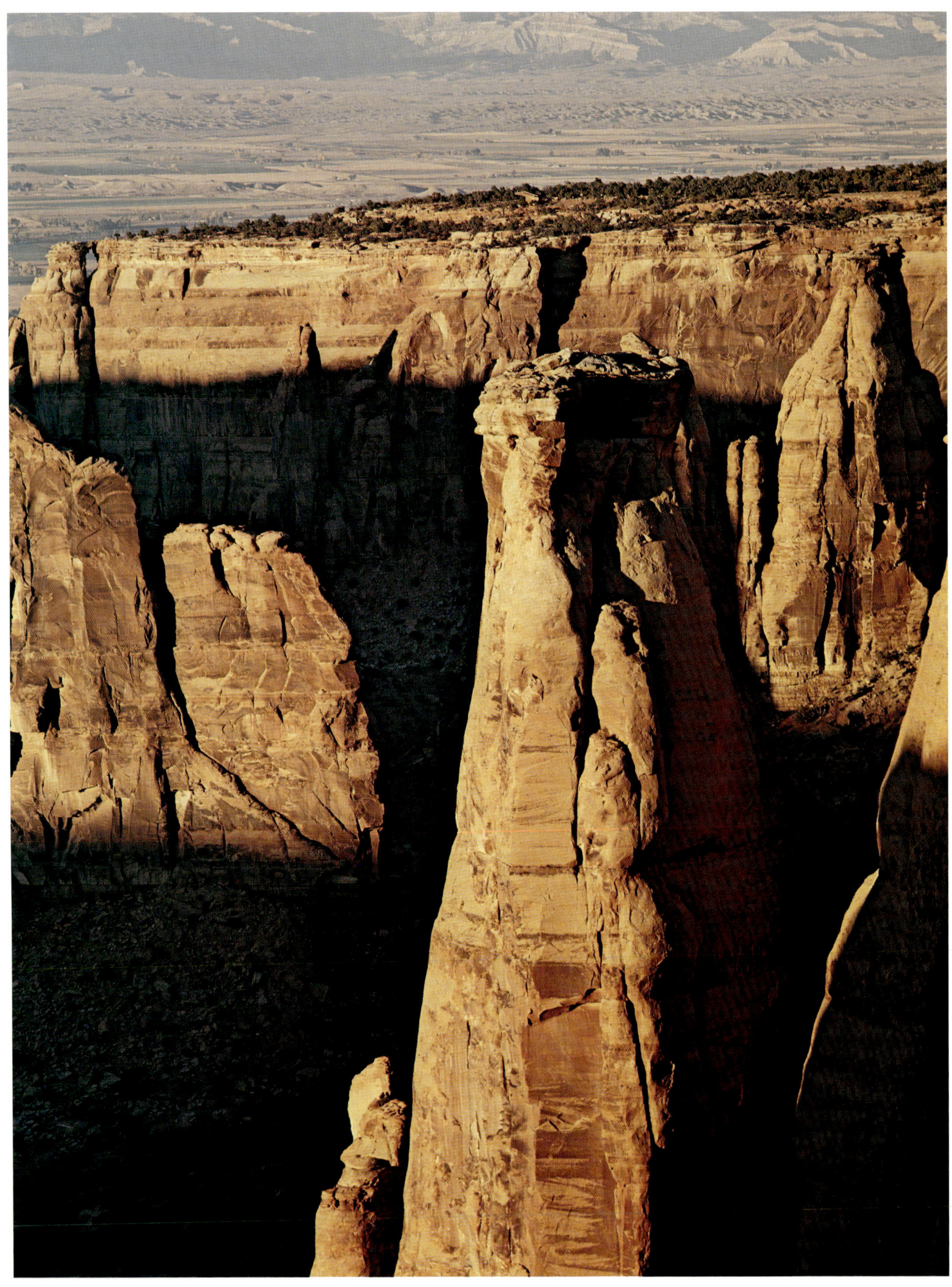

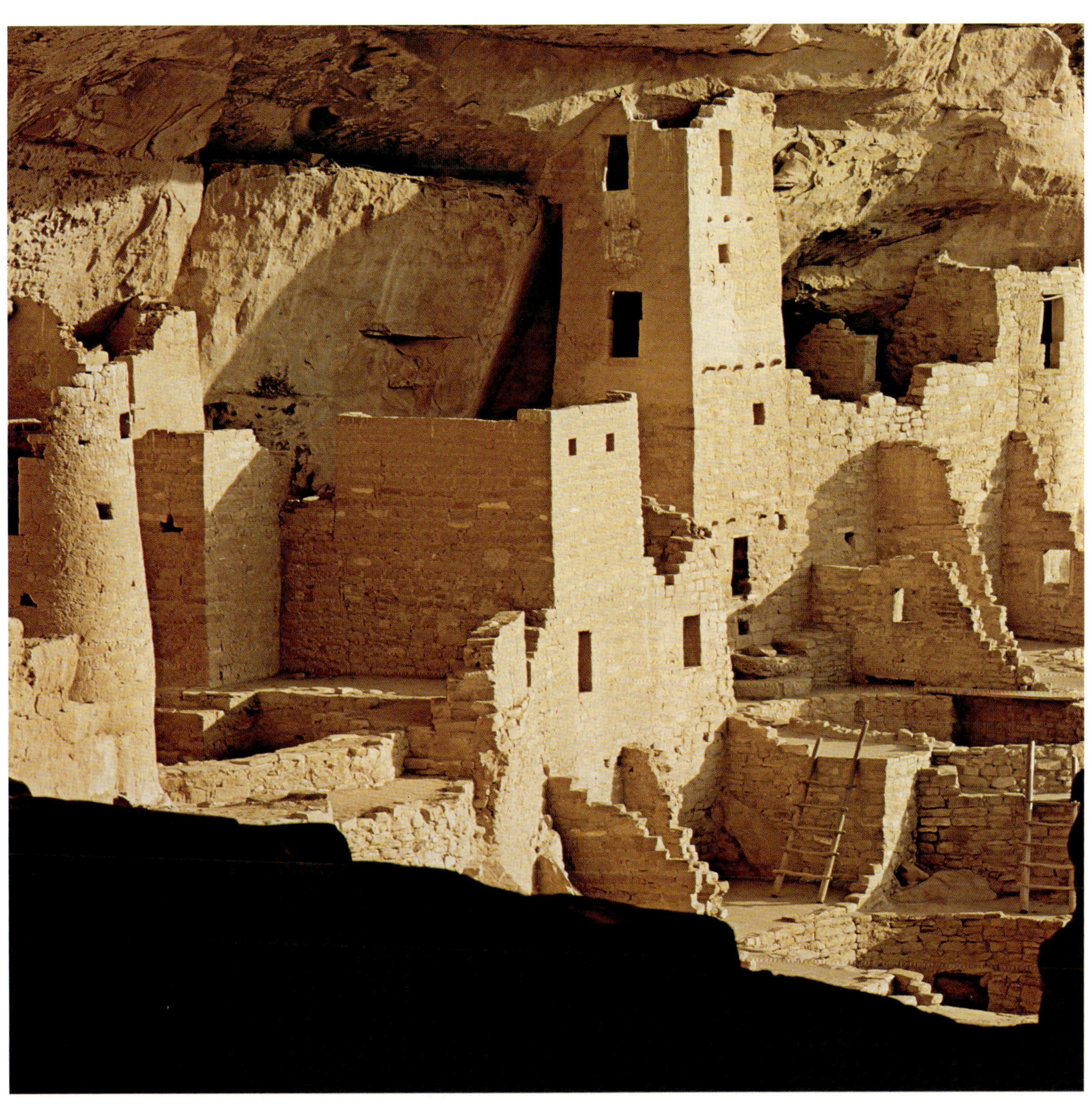

◄ Sandstone pinnacles, on Uncompahgre Plateau's northeast slope, are a feature of Colorado National Monument.
▲ Round and square towers cling to the walls of Cliff Palace at Mesa Verde.

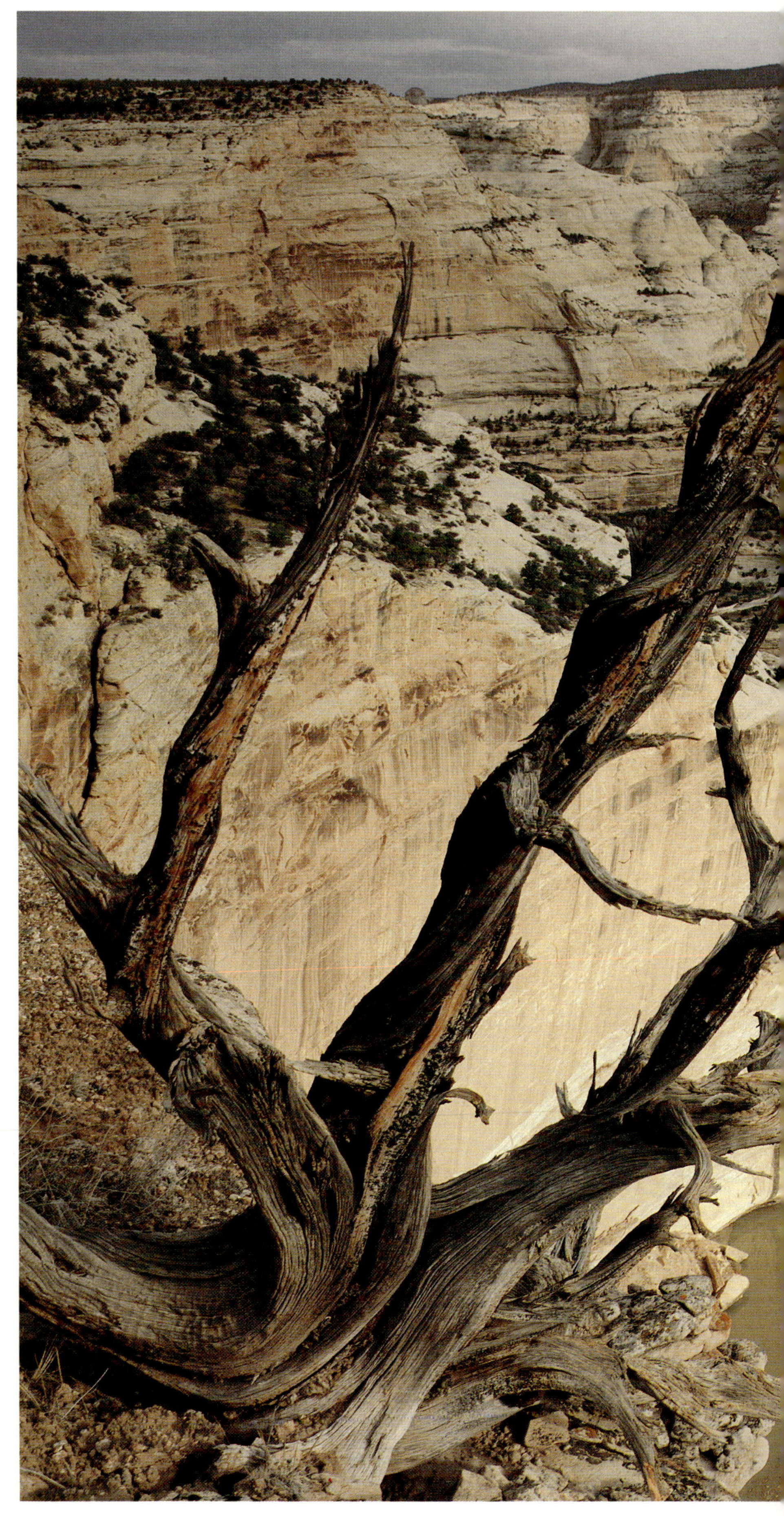

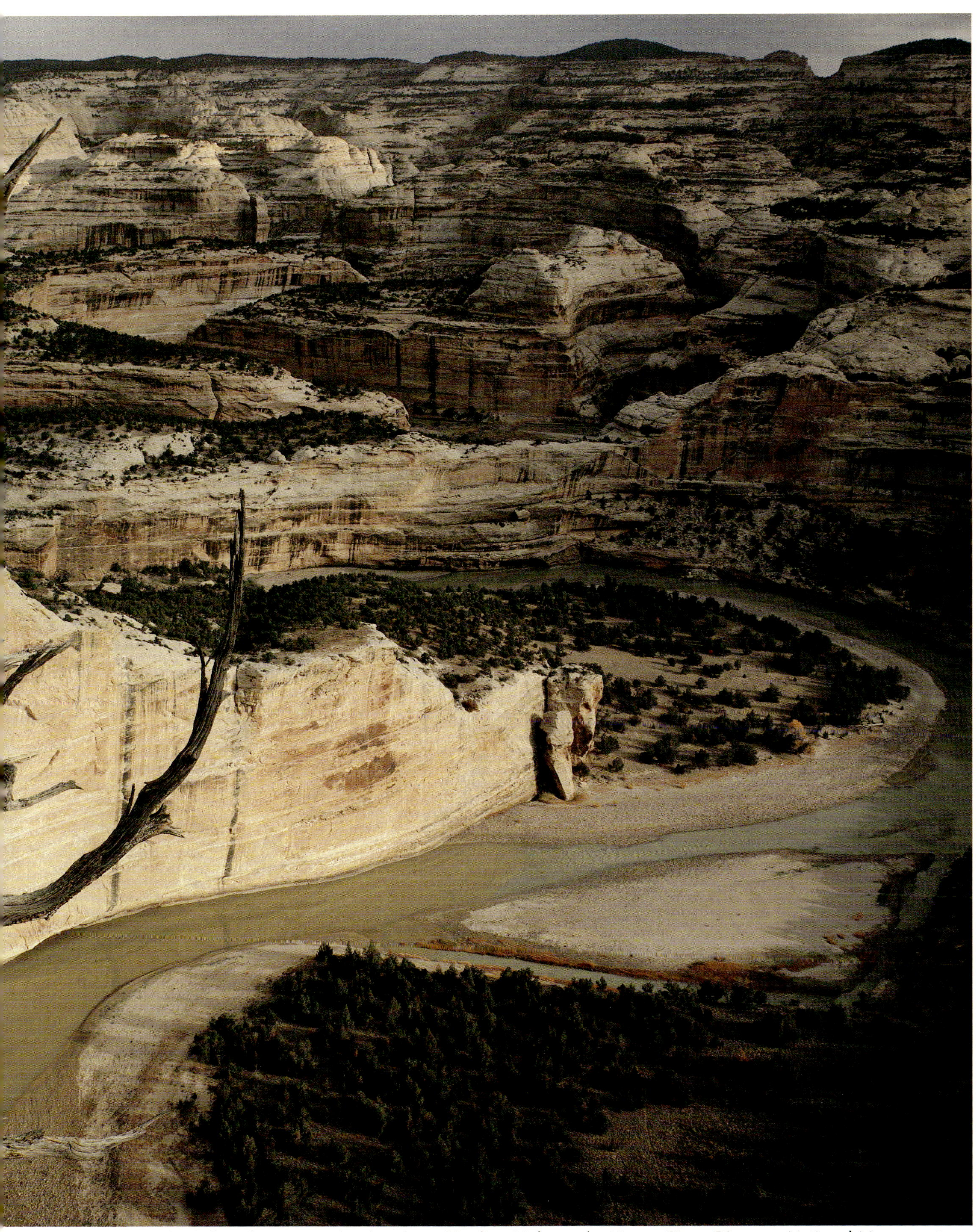

▲ A juniper ghost leans over the rim above Harding Hole on the Yampa River, Dinosaur National Monument.

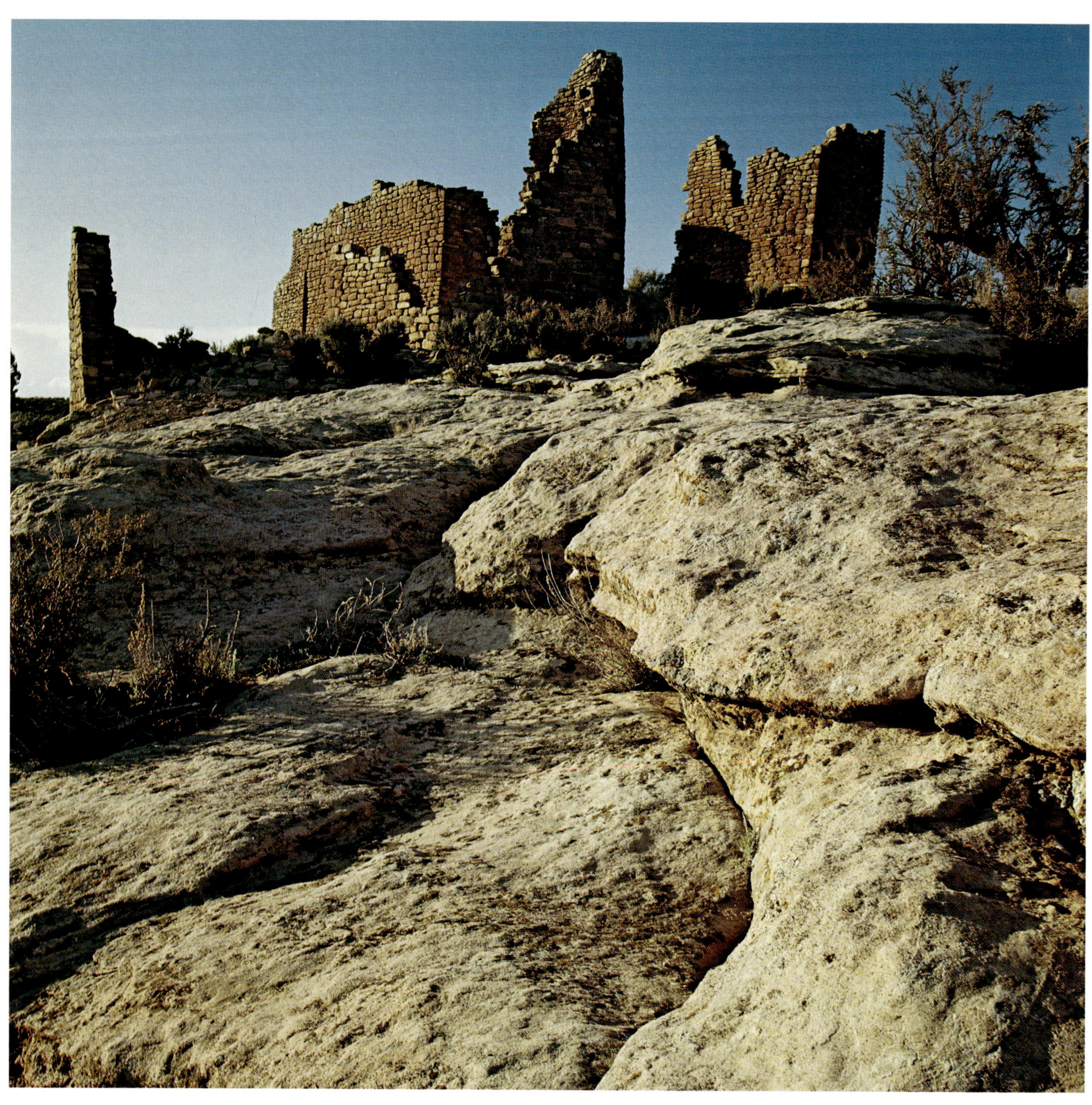

▲ Prehistoric Indian ruins, occupied around 1200 A.D., make up Hovenweep National Monument.
► At this 2,000-foot depth, in Black Canyon of the Gunnison, the sun only strikes for a few minutes each day.

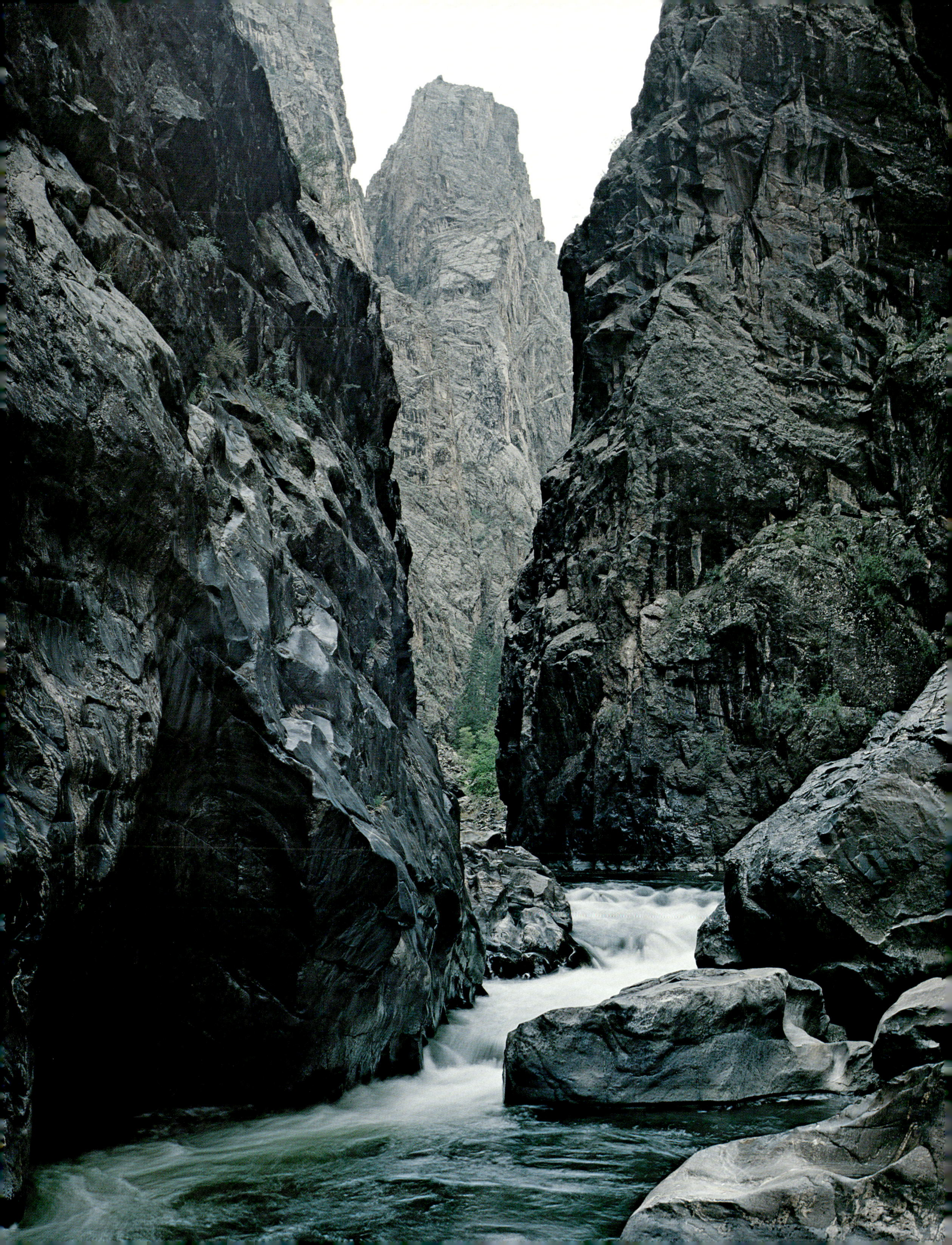

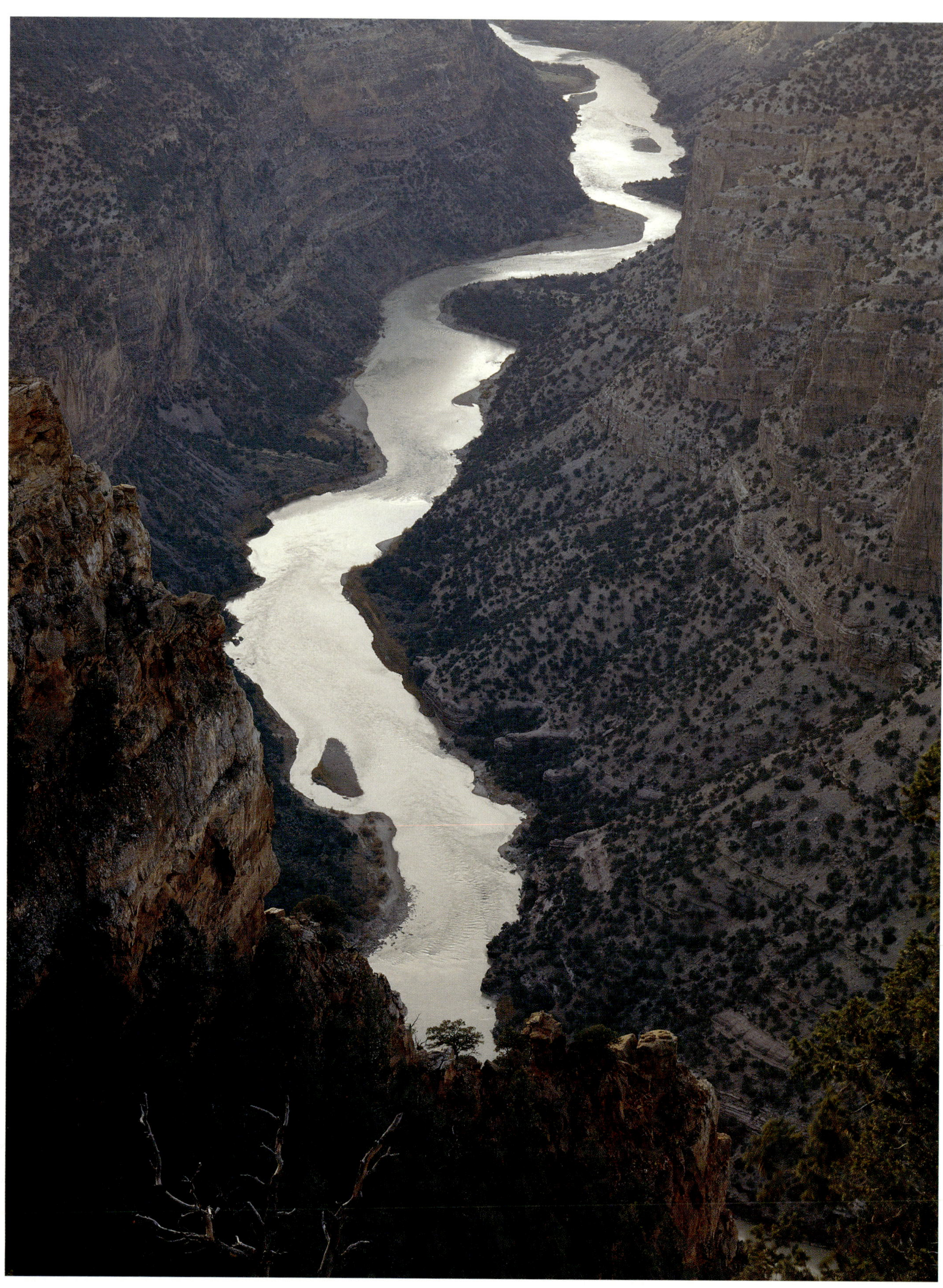

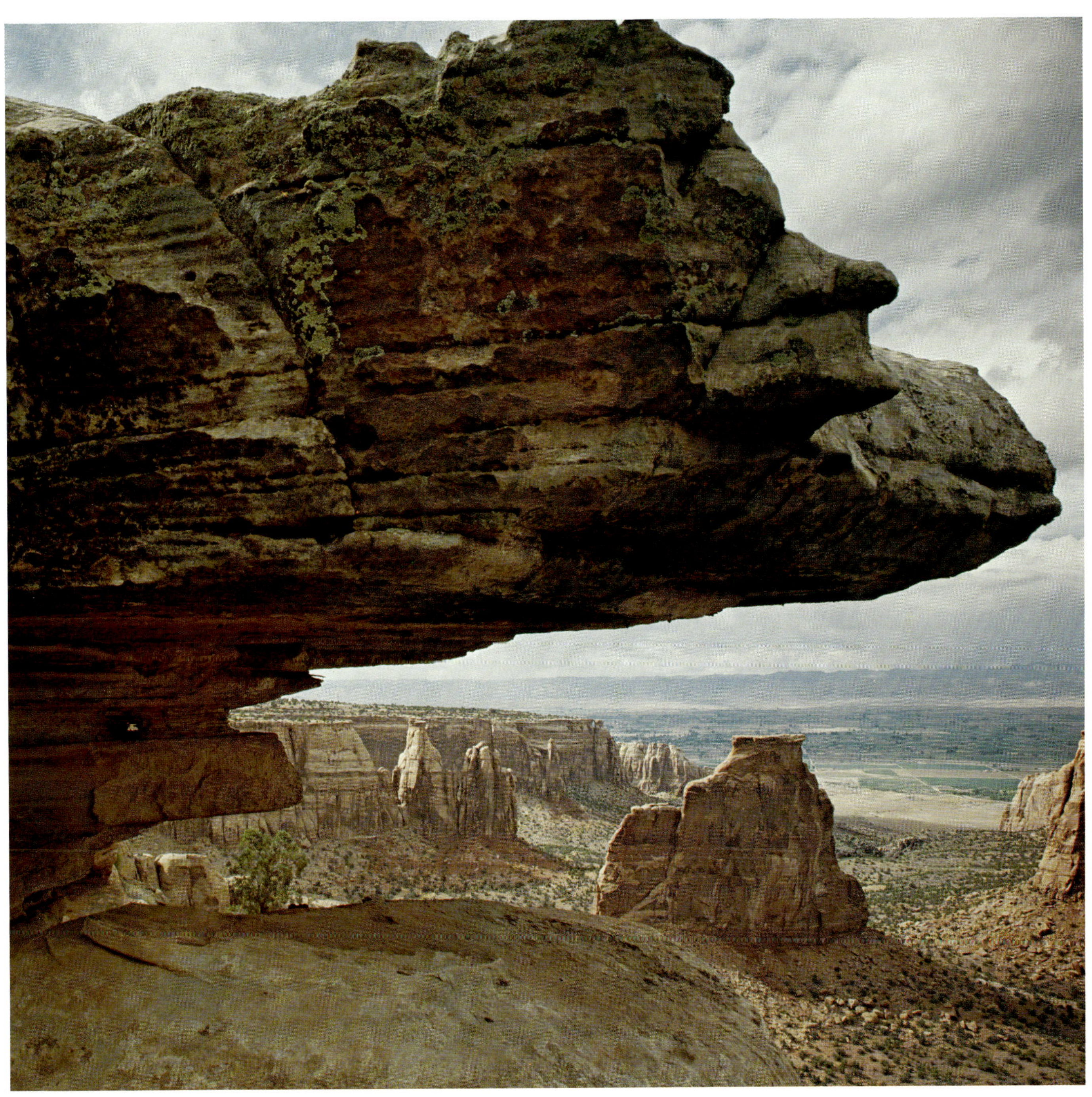

◄ Green River pours into Whirlpool Canyon, cut from shale and limestone rock in Dinosaur National Monument.
▲ Massive sandstone outcroppings rim the valley at Colorado National Monument.

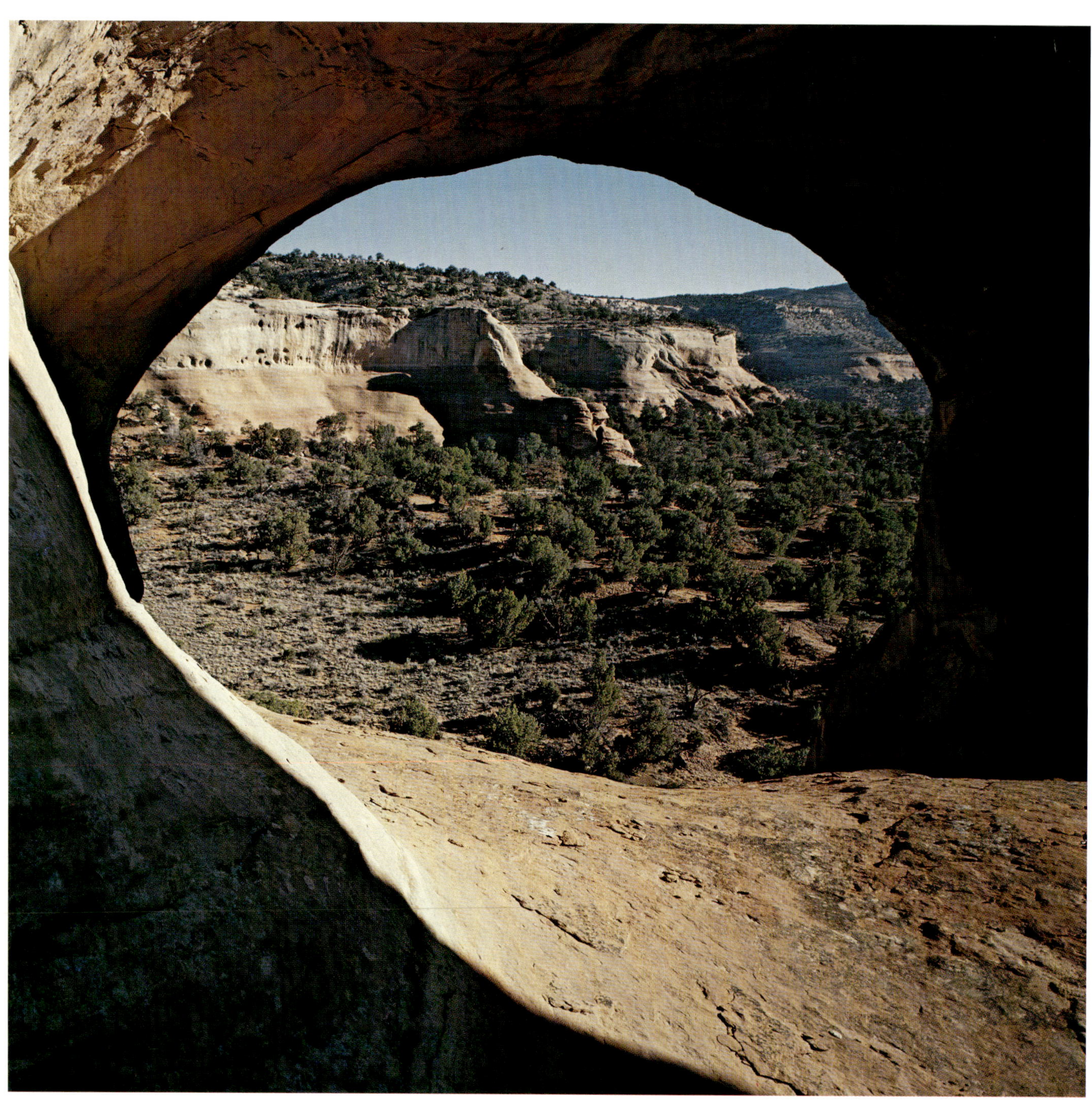

▲ Rainbow Arch is one of the many arches in Rattlesnake Canyon, on the Uncompahgre Plateau.

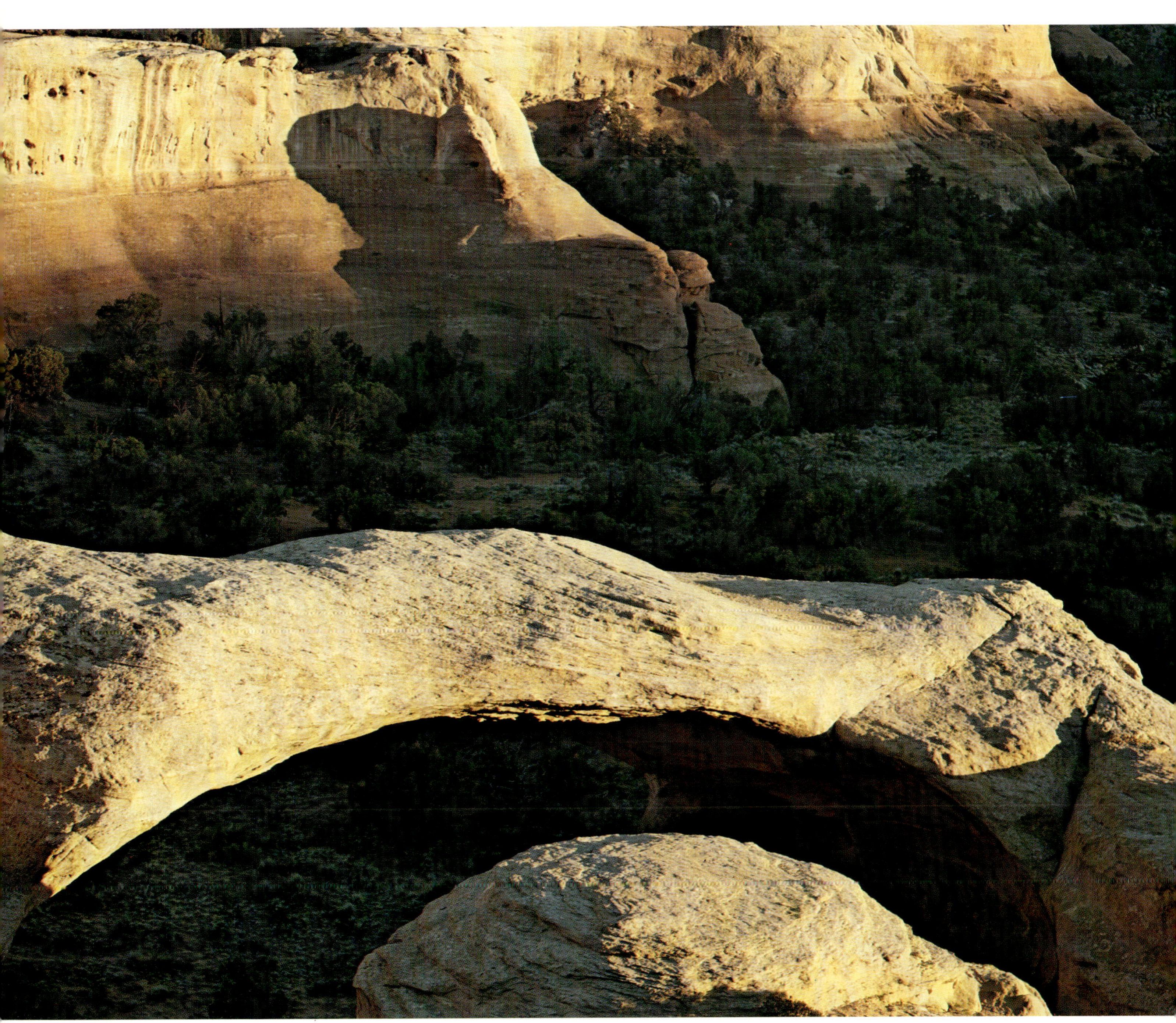

▲ Elements of wind and water and time have carved and eroded these sandstones on the Uncompahgre Plateau.

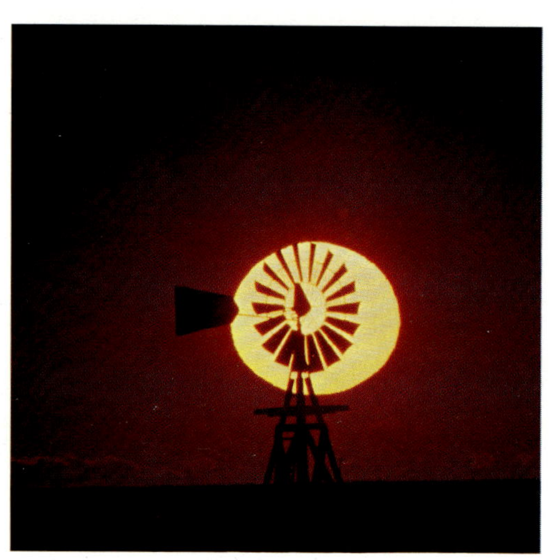

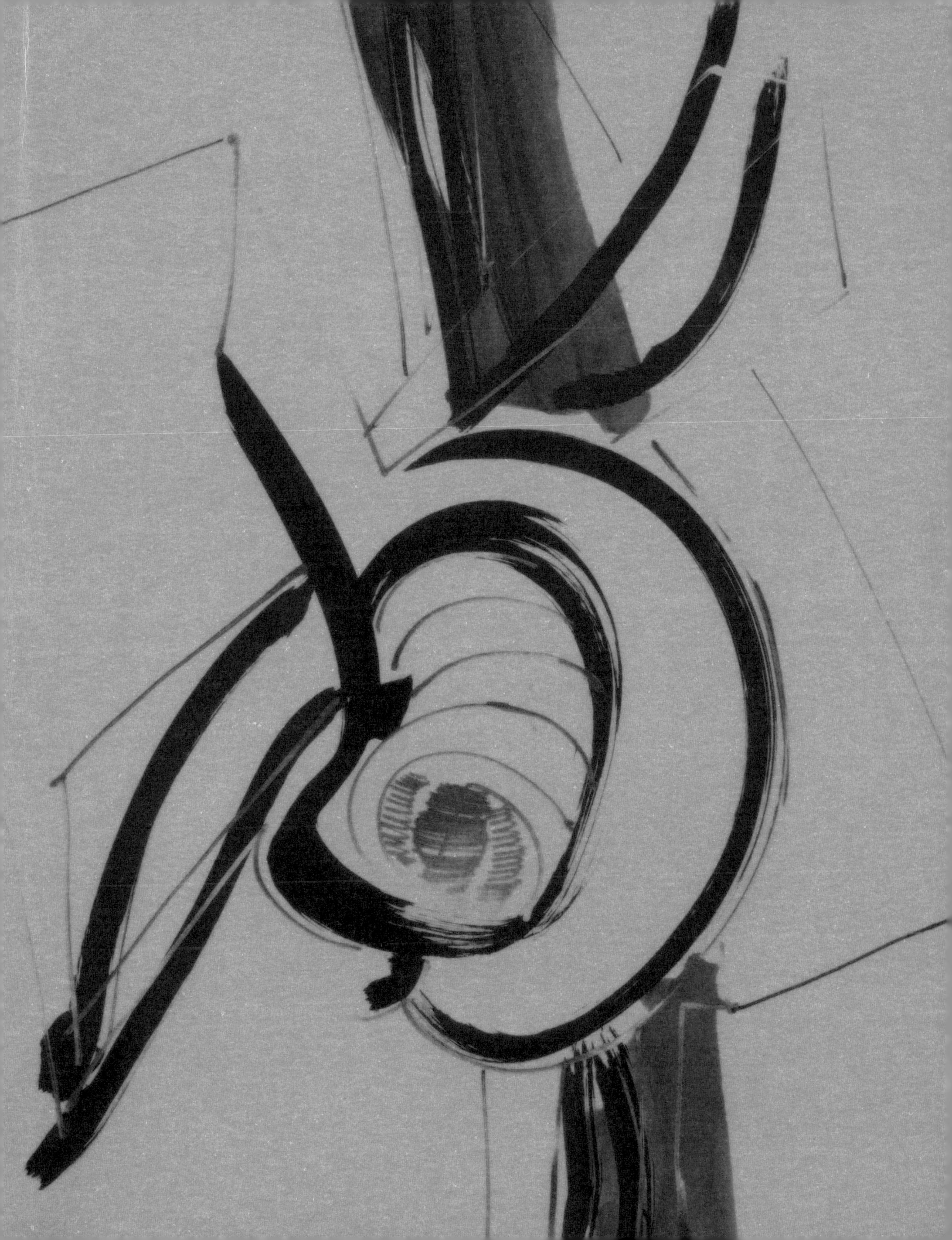

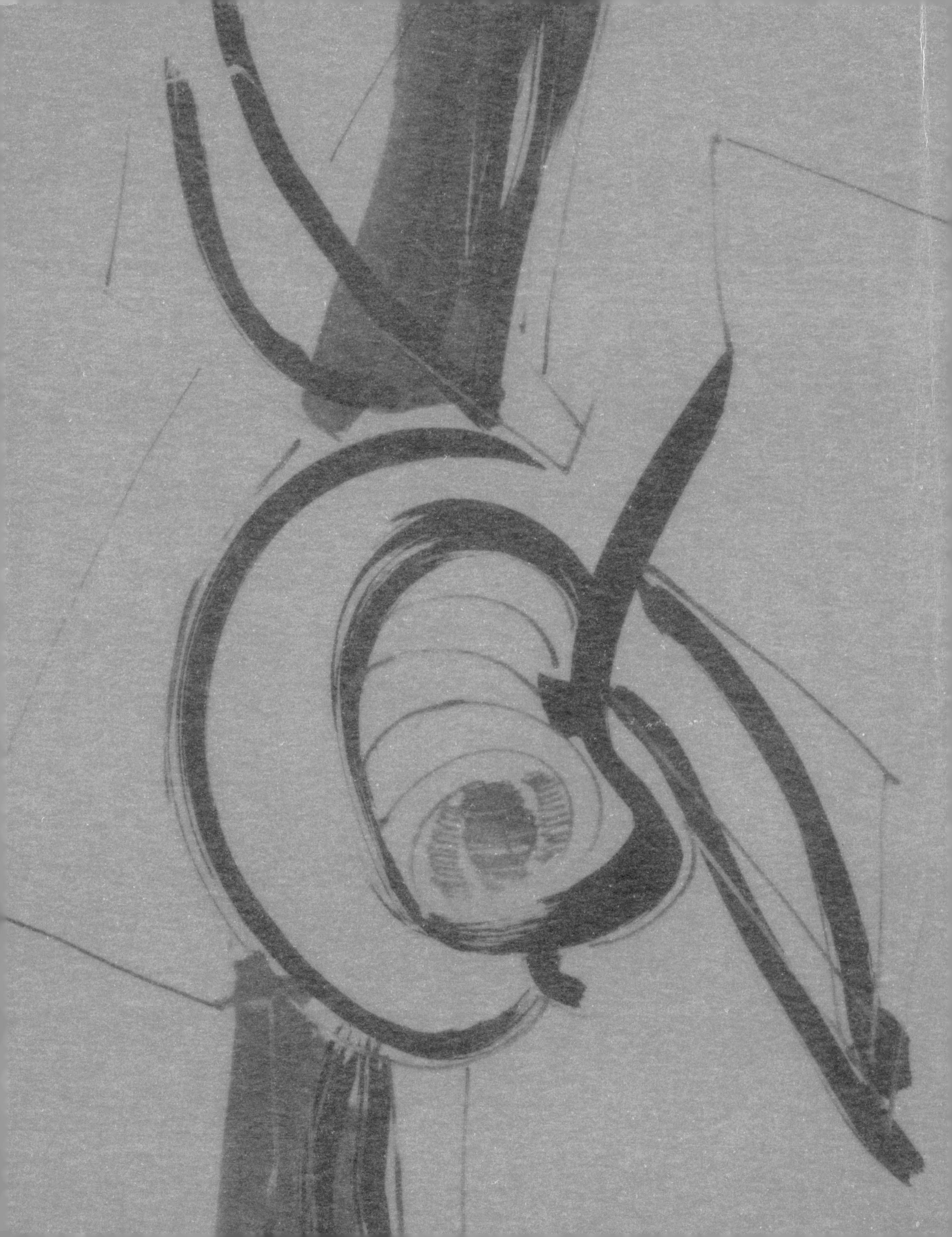